PITTSBURGH IRISH

Erin on the Three Rivers

GERARD F. O'NEIL

Foreword by Diane O. Byrnes

The History PRESS

Published by The History Press
Charleston, SC 29403
www.historypress.net

Front cover, bottom: Cox's Army at Wilkinsburg, Pennsylvania.
Courtesy of St. Patrick–St. Stanislaus Kostka Parish Archives.

First published 2015

Manufactured in the United States

ISBN 978.1.62619.829.6

Library of Congress Control Number: 2015942274

To all our predecessors, in both the old world and the new, who are now forgotten.

CONTENTS

CONTENTS

FOREWORD

Dear Readers,

Allow me to introduce Gerry O'Neil—teacher, student, sound engineer, gardener, historian and author. I first met Mr. O'Neil many years ago at Rosebud, a music venue that was located in Pittsburgh's Strip District. Mr. O'Neil was the sound engineer for an Irish group performing there, and while I cannot recall the name of the band, I could never forget Gerry O'Neil. Gerry came highly recommended when, as a concert promoter, I needed a sound engineer for a variety of events and venues. Gerry is the man; he makes the music sound the way it should. Whether it's folk, rock or ethnic, Gerry O'Neil continues to make the sounds of music ever so pleasant.

Over the twenty-five years I have worked with Gerry, a friendship has developed through our many intellectually stimulating conversations on a broad range of topics. Whatever we discussed, though, history was always involved. I was constantly impressed with Gerry's knowledge on so many topics, especially his knowledge of Irish things, which brings me to this book: *Pittsburgh Irish: Erin on the Three Rivers*. I am not surprised that Gerry decided to write about the Irish; for a very long time, Gerry has had a sense of times past and the Irish. Of course, with a last name like O'Neil, he could be a distant descendant of Niall of the Nine Hostages (the alleged pirate who captured St. Patrick and brought him to Ireland).

While the Pittsburgh region has a rich history that includes many groups of immigrants, this book concentrates on Irish immigrants and all they brought (and continue to bring) to this region. Starting in the early 1700s, Gerry takes us through the early migration of the Irish from Ulster, the northernmost province of the island. Many of these settlers were descendants of the lowland Scots, Welsh and English peoples who were "planted" in the north of Ireland during the reign of Elizabeth I in the 1600s.

Upon immigration to southwestern Pennsylvania, these Irish folks brought with them their hopes and dreams for a better life. They brought their work ethic and their language, much of which has been absorbed into our Pittsburgh vocabulary. Their experience of tyranny and oppression back home in Ireland, coupled with a strong individualist streak and a considerable bit of stubbornness, gave these people their own sense of justice and rights. We see these assertive tendencies in the Whiskey Rebellion that eventually contributed to the creation of the Democratic Party, the struggle for recognition of unions and the many battles with bigotry. In short, the Irish are people who helped shape America.

Mr. O'Neil has assembled a well-developed timeline of the migration of the Irish to southwestern Pennsylvania that informs us from whence they came and where they settled. Who were these Irish, and how did they benefit this land? They were farmers and tradesmen; they built railroads and canals across the land; they were miners and union leaders. Irish women were housewives, maids, factory workers and union activists. They brought religion with them as well, and many of these first immigrants were Presbyterians who were well educated and had a variety of skill sets and a bit of money; many others, however, were peasants, weavers and political exiles. All were ready to call the new land home. There were many pathways from Ireland, and each group brought something different. Many of these folks brought their fiddles and whistles, and even today you can hear the "Irish" in the music of the Appalachians. In fact, a huge Irish influence can be heard in traditional American music across historical eras.

As the young nation continued to expand, Irish Presbyterians, mostly from Ulster, pushed the frontier west, helping to found the city of Pittsburgh and leaving place and family names all over the map: Donegal, Derry, Tyrone, Strabane and so on. Within the city of Pittsburgh, there appeared notable pockets or settlements of people from Limerick and Galway, while Irish shantytowns sprang up like mushrooms along railroads and in mining camps. The arrival of Irish Catholics in large numbers between 1820 and 1840 stirred up controversy and resentment in Pittsburgh. Although the response to a perceived Papist threat was not as violent as it was in eastern Pennsylvania, immigrants were often unwelcome, except as a source of cheap labor. Nonetheless, these Irish Catholic women and men quickly established hospitals, fraternal organizations and the college that became Duquesne University.

The advent of the Civil War provided an opportunity for the Irish to demonstrate valor, patriotism and/or mercenary spirit, a model for "becoming American" that has been followed by many subsequent waves of immigrants. A few western Pennsylvanians joined Pennsylvania's 166th Regiment of the Irish Brigade, but most Irishmen fought and died with locally recruited regiments that drew on many ethnic communities. Irish women died, too—a massive explosion at the Allegheny Arsenal highlighted the dangers of working in the emergent "arsenal of democracy." The life of Charles F. McKenna, a Civil War soldier who saw over twenty engagements and went on to become a judge and pillar of the Pittsburgh community for decades, illustrates the Irish transition to the mainstream of American society.

Not all Irish-Americans rose to prominence quickly, however. Most found work in factories, built railroads or were servants. Later, Irishmen were promoted to shop foremen over Eastern European immigrants, elevations that became a source of frequent conflict that mill owners attempted to use to their advantage. Irish workers played a prominent role in the long struggle to organize unions in Pittsburgh. Moreover, the Irish were renowned for being both hardworking and hard drinking; the lore of the mines and mills contains a number of anecdotes and jokes reflecting this reputation. Yet the Irish community also included a strong movement of teetotalers, with a particularly Irish Catholic twist—an aversion to prohibition, instead favoring moral persuasion and example. In Pittsburgh, this abstention movement reflected the pre-immigration background of many Irishmen who were skilled tradesmen and occupied the middle rungs of the economic ladder before moving to Pittsburgh—not all immigrants were penniless peasants. Labor unions and secret societies, such as Clan na Gael, also supported temperance because drunkenness undermined discipline in the ranks.

In the twentieth century, Pittsburgh's Irish population became firmly ensconced in American culture and politics while many moved up the economic ladder. At the same time, new arrivals from the "ould sod" have continued to find a new home in Pittsburgh. The era after World War II also saw the emergence of a number of foundations and institutions designed both to strengthen cultural and economic ties with Ireland and to support the Irish nation's development—often by giving individuals a chance to live and work in Pittsburgh.

FOREWORD

There are so many facts in this book of which I was not aware, and I know a lot about Irish history in America, so Gerry's book is an excellent learning tool, as well as a good read. It is interesting to note, for instance, that the Ancient Order of Hibernians formed an early chapter in Pittsburgh in the late 1840s and then to realize that this organization is still a very strong and effective society of men and women around America, especially in Pittsburgh. The history and lore of Pittsburgh features many colorful Irish pastors and politicians, rebels and radicals, saints and sinners, and some selected individuals fall into several of these categories. Pittsburgh's more (in)famous Irishmen and women give us another window into Irish Pittsburgh. Gerry O'Neil has put his knowledge, his research and his organizational skills to excellent use in writing this book. You, the reader, will take away new perspectives and information on the development of our region by Irish immigrants, and perhaps *Pittsburgh Irish* will encourage you to pursue further learning on Irish history, culture, music, poetry, politics and everything else Irish.

Respectfully,

Diane O. Byrnes
Producer and Host
Echoes of Erin on WEDO 810AM
(Irish radio programming)

ACKNOWLEDGEMENTS

First and foremost, I would like to thank Janis R. Ferrainolo, my partner in everything, including the stresses of writing my first book. When an excerpt failed the "Janis at 11:00 p.m. test," it was not yet ready for any other reader.

I would like to thank Ted McGraw for preserving and making available the "Fardowns" song and Terra Merkey, the music librarian at Duquesne University's Gumberg Library, who handled a number of arcane requests.

I would also like to thank Pittsburgh-area archives and their staff: David Grinnell and Miriam Meislik at the University of Pittsburgh's Archives Service Center; Matthew Strauss at the John Heinz History Center, Detre Library and Archives; Donna Meyers at the Dunbar Historical Society and Steve Gluz for his painting of the Dunbar mine disaster; Reverend Harry Nichols and Derris Jeffcoat at St. Patrick–St. Stanislaus Kostka Parish; Michael Kraus at the Soldiers and Sailors Memorial Hall Archives; Gilbert Pietrzak at the Pennsylvania Room, Carnegie Library, Oakland; and Bruce Klein at the Museum of Photo Antiquities.

I appreciate the support and guidance of Thomas White, Duquesne University archivist and prolific History Press author. Special thanks to Dr. Perry Blatz and Dr. Joseph Rishel, who contributed their expertise and research leads on Pittsburgh's past—may you continue to enjoy your retirements from Duquesne University.

Special thanks to my crew of readers at the La Roche College Writers' Center: led by the intrepid Dr. Christine Abbott, along with Rebecca

Loestetter, Katelynn Gazarik and Clay Malone, with additional thanks to my "prefrooder," Janis R. Ferrainolo.

I would like to thank Liz Shovlin Grinko for bringing me up to speed on the origins of Irish dance schools in Pittsburgh and providing some classic pictures. Special thanks also to Jim Lamb of the Ireland Institute for explaining its activities over the years and providing images. Thanks to Terry Griffith for ideas, promotion and always having at hand a good rebel song. Further thanks to Janis R. Ferrainolo for traveling far and wide for contemporary photos. I would also like to thank Maureen McIntyre at the Carnegie Historical Society for providing both clarity and some local family-based history of the Klan riot. Thanks to Gerard Rohlf for songs and ideas to help drive my story and "Fare Thee Well Newlanders."

I would be remiss if I did not thank Diane Byrnes for promoting Irish music and introducing me to the Pittsburgh Irish music scene nearly twenty-five years ago. A further shout-out to all the Irish musicians I have worked with in this city, including but not limited to: current and former members of Guaranteed Irish, Red Hand Paddy, the Wild Geese, Corned Beef & Curry, Whiskey Limerick, the Rivermen, Celtic Fringe, Donnie Irish, Hooley, Bastard Bearded Irishmen and solo performers far too numerous to mention. Omissions here should not be taken as an offense.

Finally, thanks to the entire community in Pittsburgh, Irish or not, that continues to celebrate and commemorate the city of Pittsburgh's unique heritage.

Did I remember to thank Janis R. Ferrainolo?

INTRODUCTION

This book is a rather bold undertaking. The history of Pittsburgh, while short by European standards, is nonetheless both complex and rich. The story of the Irish peoples and their scattered communities across the globe is vast and inherently unmanageable as a coherent narrative, yet I hereby endeavor to examine only a tiny Pittsburgh-focused slice of Irish and American history. The result is a set of vignettes or snapshots that tell the story of Irish Pittsburgh.

When people think of the Irish in America, the large industrial cities come to mind: New York, Chicago, Boston—places where Irish immigrants have long been a formidable political force. Yet Pittsburgh has a significant Irish tradition, and a strong one, reflected in the fact that today Pittsburgh hosts the second-largest St. Patrick's Day parade in America. This book will address that tradition and the history of the Irish people in and around the Steel City. We will look at the adventures of the Irish west of the Alleghenies with an emphasis on the "Greater Pittsburgh Region," best defined as Allegheny County and the six surrounding counties: Butler, Westmoreland, Washington, Beaver, Fayette and Lawrence. For the purpose of my story, and in the interests of improved historical perspective, Pittsburgh should not be sundered from its hinterlands—that is, the surrounding regions that have always fed the city with raw materials while benefiting, in turn, from the goods and services found in a metropolis.

On St. Patrick's Day, everyone is Irish, apparently. The other 364.25 days of the year, notions of Irish identity are contested. Many of these divisions are, to a great extent, a post-colonial artifact that I wish to sidestep as much as possible, if the reader will indulge me. The leaders of the British Empire, like all successful imperialists, went beyond the practice of divide and conquer by provoking new divisions that enabled them to retain conquered territory. In 1609, the English King Charles I forcibly removed the O'Neill and O'Donnell clans from the north of Ireland and then imported twenty thousand English and Scottish Protestants to found the Plantation of Ulster. Essentially, the British took two problems (from their perspective) and created a third one: "settling" troublesome Presbyterians from Scotland in the northern part of Ireland had enduring results.

Arguments over "authenticity" also reflect a divide between recent immigrants and the thoroughly Americanized descendants of earlier immigrants. Green beer, for instance, is a rather pathetic American invention that speaks volumes about commercialism and the shallowness of American culture but tells us little about Irish tradition. Few people today know that the words to the supposedly quintessential Irish song "Danny Boy" were actually written by Frederic Weatherly, an English lawyer. Contemporary Irish songwriter Robbie O'Connell sings, "You're not Irish," as he criticizes this tension between perceived notions of Irish authenticity:

You're not Irish you can't be Irish you don't know Danny Boy
Or Toora Loora Loola, or even Irish eyes
You've got the hell of a nerve to say you came from Ireland
So cut out all the nonsense and sing McNamara's Band

Traditionally, and perhaps stereotypically, the Irish have displayed a penchant for disagreement both with outsiders and among ourselves. So let's not start another here. Arguments about who is "really" Irish have a limited place in this story of Irish Pittsburgh.

Perhaps the problem for all historians is that humans so often prefer certainty and simple, uncomplicated narratives. In this case, the notion of the Irish as a monolithic cultural entity is a limited, oversimplified and incomplete story. Most narratives emphasize the urban experience, as if no Irishmen ever took up farming on the new sod. Often, in the American story, the terms "Irish" and "Catholic" are interchangeable, but the history of Pittsburgh shows that this conflation can be misleading. A number of Protestants came from Ireland, and many of the early Catholic arrivals to Pittsburgh were of German origin. Indeed the narrative of Irish assimilation into the American melting pot overlooks many people. The emphasis on

Catholic lower-class men fleeing the Famine of '47 overlooks the stories of Protestants, antebellum and pre-famine immigrants, women and skilled tradesmen. It has been argued that Irish Protestants rapidly abandoned their Irish identity in favor of a Protestant one—to the point of participating in anti-Catholic riots.

The craving for simple narratives partially explains the tendency to overlook early nineteenth-century immigrants, including Catholics. Irish women, underrepresented as well, were less likely to be literate and were not priests, politicians or influential in trade and commerce. The reasons for overlooking Irish skilled tradesmen are unclear, but stereotyping of the poor Irish certainly played a part. Two important facts about narratives must be kept in mind: they serve the interests of the dominant culture, but they are constantly in the process of renegotiation. This book is a small piece of the re-negotiation process; it attempts to include previously ignored groups, such as Irish Presbyterians.

And finally, perhaps any narrative about "how the Irish became American" is akin to looking through the wrong end of a telescope. It may be just as revealing to ask "how America became Irish." Author Danny Cassidy, while not supported by an extensive body of scholars, has pointed to the possibility that much of American vernacular, or slang, is of Gaelic origin. Historian James Barrett explains how, as America's "first ethnic group," the Irish defined the immigrant experience for future waves of immigrants in the fields of economics, religion and politics. Another historian, Cian T. McMahon (a former Pittsburgh resident), suggests that the Irish in America were not primarily motivated to "become White"; that is, to assimilate themselves into the dominant Anglo-centric culture, as argued by Noel Ignatiev. Instead, Irish immigrants in Pittsburgh have long viewed themselves as part of a global and transnational "imagined community." Indeed, many of the images selected for inclusion in this book show how Pittsburgh's Irish imagined themselves as part of a transnational community that was a consequence of the Irish diaspora. In this tentative spirit of inquiry, then, we shall examine Pittsburgh through the Irish imagination. Analysis, theories and evaluation of evidence are all necessary parts of the historian's toolkit, but at the end of the day (and some overlong nights), we are storytellers. I hope you enjoy this one.

Part I

THE PENNSYLVANIA FRONTIER

Rogues, Rebels and the Respectable, 1717–1820

We shall start with the naming of places and people. Names are a fascinating subject of historical study. The act of naming isolates one particular place or people from the rest of the world and says, "This is different." At the same time, naming a place after a previous abode creates connections and suggests continuity. The power of this process helps explain why, for instance, there are four Donegals in southwestern Pennsylvania and several more closer to Philadelphia. Other western Pennsylvania names pointing back to northern Ireland include Armagh, Derry, Rostraver, Menallen and Tyrone, to name but a few.

The naming of people, on the other hand, can be far more contentious. Names attempt to convey powerful and incompletely examined notions of identity that have emerged from particular historical circumstances. Anyone who values tolerance can see the limitations inherent in the convenient color-coded shorthand of "green" for Catholic and "orange" for Protestant that are found, respectively, on the left and right sides of the Irish flag. Apparently no one, or perhaps everyone, claims the "white" for peace and the gospel page that connects or separates the two colors on the Irish flag, depending on the perspective of the viewer.

Likewise, the use of the term "Scotch-Irish" (or Scots-Irish, as our friends across the pond would have it) is problematic from the perspective of historians. Before 1830, the term "Scotch-Irish" is rarely used as a label for self-identification, and instead there is a strong body of evidence that Irish Presbyterians in western Pennsylvania (and elsewhere in early America) regarded themselves as Irish and Presbyterian. Historian Peter Gilmore has argued that regardless of their original ancestry, "Presbyterians who left Ireland did so for Irish reasons, their values, politics and aspirations shaped by Irish history and experience." Pittsburgh's earliest St. Patrick's Day parades, which, of course, included the obligatory Robert Burns songs, were largely run by Irish-born Presbyterians, as were early Irish fraternal organizations. Rather than engage in a lengthy digression on identity politics or research methodologies, I will point to the words of Pittsburgh's Irish historian Peter Gilmore:

> *The construction of a Scotch-Irish identity recast the term's meaning in ways that changed the humble hyphen from a connecting bridge to a concrete wall topped with barbed wire. The assertion of identity has generally been understood to be both a late nineteenth-century, middle class Protestant response to the mass immigration of poor, unruly Catholic Irish and an attempt by upwardly mobile individuals of Ulster background to retroactively certify the respectability of their social origins.*

For these reasons, I will borrow Gilmore's term "Irish Presbyterians" to refer to Irish Presbyterians. Consequently, this book will avoid the term "Scotch-Irish," except where it appears in original sources. Finally, to make the point by comparison, it would be ridiculous to claim that Irish leader Eamon de Valera wasn't "really Irish" because he was born in New York City and/or that he should be labeled "Spanish-Irish" because of his father's ancestry.

From Ireland into the Wilderness

As many as 500,000 immigrants arrived in America from Ireland between 1680 and 1830; most were from Ulster. They left from the major ports of Derry and Belfast and from smaller ports in Donegal. As a result, western Pennsylvania is sprinkled with Irish place names today. The majority of these immigrants were Presbyterians of Scottish ancestry, but some were native Irish converts to Protestant denominations and native Irish Catholics. In short, there is no simple narrative. There were five great waves of migration to America from the northern regions of Ireland between 1717 and 1775. Drought, high rents, poverty, famine, religious persecution and political restrictions compelled Ulster Presbyterians to seek a better life in Penn's colony. In Ireland, a series of statutes, collectively known as the Penal Laws, sharply restricted the freedoms and economic activities of Presbyterians as well as Catholics, and the Test Act required all officeholders to take a test that affirmed their conformity to Anglican doctrine. Effective propaganda by the Penn family's agents and letters written home from America by earlier migrants contributed to chain migration.

The linen trade had long connected Philadelphia with Ireland, and William Penn's Quaker colony promoted religious tolerance. Unlike many other colonies, Pennsylvania was a place where Presbyterians would not be required to pay a tithe to a state-sanctioned established church. Presbyterians dominated Irish immigration until approximately 1830, and most sought not wealth but independence as farmers. Ultimately, they transported a pre-capitalist European peasant culture defined in religious and ethnic terms, yet this culture was broadly similar to that of their Catholic contemporaries. Peter Gilmore points to a shared world of "magical charms and enchanted stills; impartible inheritance, endogamous marriage, customary whiskey production; agrarian protest and antagonism towards Episcopalian landlords; and also, an attachment to republicanism and Irish patriotic symbols." In short, Irish immigrants had much in common, whatever their religious denominations.

A distinctive characteristic of rural Irish culture was that a man was subservient to his father until his father's death, and only at that point did the land pass to the next generation; thus, a sixty-year-old man remained a landless "boy" as long as his father was still alive. Traditions varied, but in much of Ireland, younger sons did not have the opportunity to inherit land eventually, leaving them several choices: working on someone else's land, serving in the military or clergy or migrating to places like western Pennsylvania in search of their own land. Single Irish women also availed themselves of the chance to leave an impoverished and paternalistic society that limited their opportunities.

At this time, most Irish immigrants to Pennsylvania arrived in Philadelphia and New Castle, Delaware. Earlier settlers had taken the best land, so they migrated through the forests and eventually across the Allegheny Mountains into the upper tributaries of the Ohio River. Roads built by General Braddock (from Cumberland, Virginia) and General Forbes (from Carlisle, Pennsylvania) made wagon passage over the mountains possible but not easy. Today, we see Pittsburgh surrounded by suburbs and rural hinterlands, and it is easy to assume an early settlement pattern moving outward from Pittsburgh.

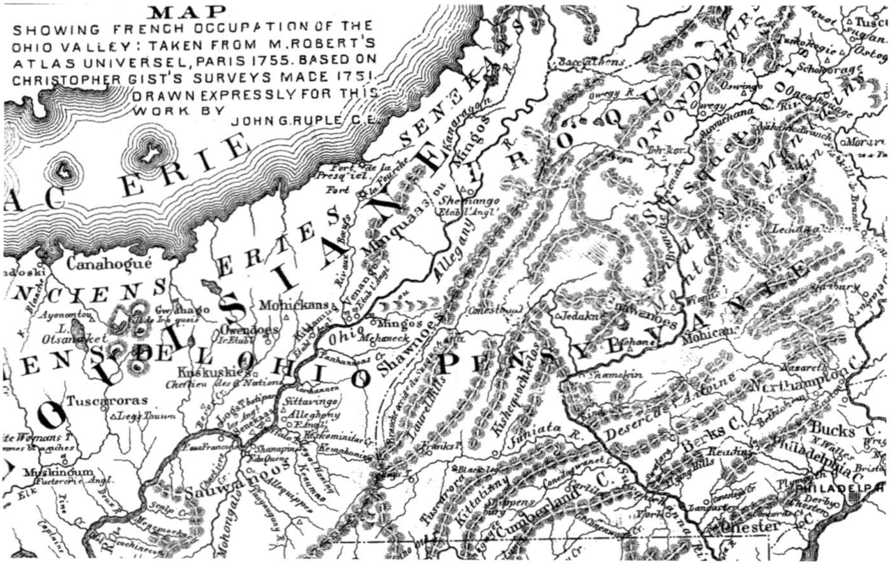

Colonial map of the three rivers, 1760. *From* "Flem's" Views of Old Pittsburgh.

However, this was not the case; early settlement was almost entirely south of Pittsburgh, and land to the north of the Ohio and Allegheny Rivers was not sold or given out until after the Revolutionary War. This settlement pattern accounts for the distribution of Irish place names, largely from Ulster, which endures to this day across the southern tier counties.

Before looking at Pittsburgh in particular, however, it is necessary to first examine the general character of the frontier settlers who pushed into the Appalachian Mountains and eventually founded communities in southwestern Pennsylvania. Notations in the genealogy of the Denny family, prestigious members of Pittsburgh's early community, reveal that, as Ulster Presbyterians, they felt they had a bad reputation to overcome. The Penn family had originally anticipated that immigrants from Ulster would make fine settlers. In fact, the Penns' agent, Secretary James Logan, wrote, "The Scotch-Irish if kindly used, will, I believe be orderly, as they have hitherto been and easily dealt with, they will also be a leading example to others." Before long, however, Logan lamented that the new arrivals were "audacious and disorderly," and he complained in 1730 that "the settlement of five families from Ireland gives me more troubles than fifty of any other people." Their rough behavior irritated neighbors to the point where, in York and Lancaster Counties, they were not permitted to buy land. They were essentially told to "move along." They did, into and over the mountains of central Pennsylvania.

Always ahead of the settlers were the fur traders. In the 1700s, the deerskin trade was huge in the Pennsylvania backcountry. Pennsylvania fur traders, led by intrepid Irishman George Croghan, had established trading posts north of the Ohio River by the 1740s and interfered in the French trade with the Miami and Huron Indians. Beavers had been all but wiped out, but there was a strong demand for deerskins in Europe. Hunting and trading sent many Irishmen deep into and beyond the Allegheny Mountains, where killing Indians and stealing their deerskins was also profitable and nearly always unpunished. The fur traders were distrusted by the frontier farmers from Ireland, who suspected the traders of supplying weapons to the Indians. A backcountry agent, Joseph Rigby, noted to his superiors at the Philadelphia trading firm of Baynton, Wharton, and Morgan, "We are surrounded by Ja-b-t-s [Jacobites?] who are continually prying into every wagon and package that comes to the gate to know the contents, and often ask whether, there is any powder or lead going back to kill the Sc-th Irishmen." In theory, the colony's profitable monopoly on trade as far west as the Ohio Valley was supposed to be orderly and peaceful, but Penn's officials did not run the trading centers at Carlisle, much less control the rough men of the backcountry.

The flow of Irish Presbyterians to the interior of Pennsylvania did not eliminate the conflict but gave it new dimensions. Generally speaking, the British government resented the fact that colonists had a tendency to steal Indian land, break treaties and provoke expensive conflicts. After the conclusion of the French and Indian War in 1763, settlers resented the fact that they were forbidden to move into the Ohio River Valley. Chief Pontiac's Rebellion, immediately following France's defeat and surrender of almost all claims to North America, was a reaction to the long-standing avarice of English-speaking settlers, who were already salivating over the land claims relinquished by the French. The rebellion was a massive and widespread strike against the English, and Fort Pitt was one of the few outposts west of the Alleghenies that did not fall to Pontiac and his allies. However, the pacifist (and, one might add, parsimonious) Quakers in Philadelphia were always reluctant to pay for troops to defend Presbyterian settlers in the mountains.

At one point, a mob/militia of Irish Presbyterian ruffians, known as the Paxton Boys, massacred innocent Conestoga Indians and even threatened to attack Philadelphia. In the subsequent war of words, Presbyterians were frequently targets of attack by Quakers and their Anglican allies as

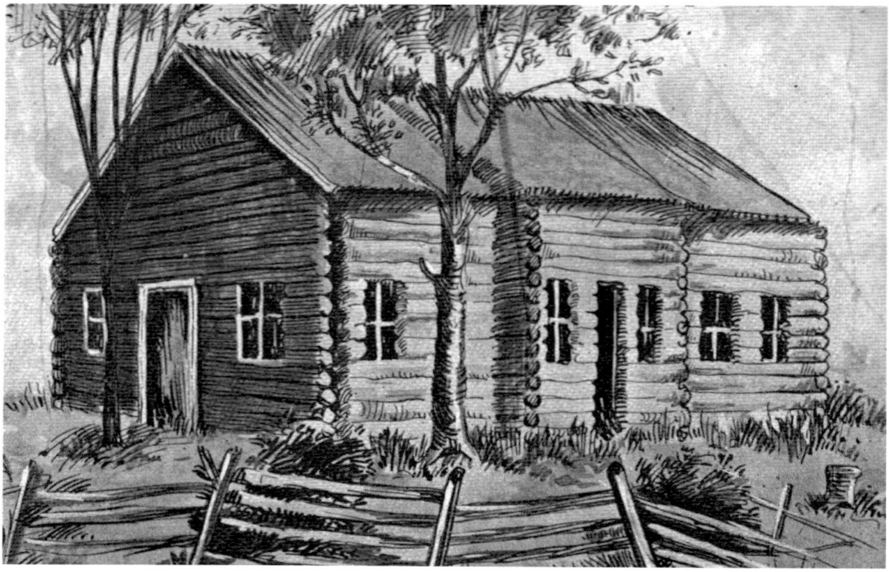

Pittsburgh's earliest Presbyterian church. *From* "Flem's" Views of Old Pittsburgh.

pamphleteering got rather vicious in Pennsylvania's pre-Revolutionary period. The image of a fanatical Presbyterian was a common stereotype in the Quakers' arguments. They were compared with Catholics and tainted with allegations of republicanism and disloyalty. A scathing and convoluted allegorical pamphlet by Anglican Isaac Hunt compared the "Piss-brute-arians" to barbaric Turks, while also linking them to both England's imperial rival, France, and England's religious adversary, Roman Catholicism. All to no avail: the Quakers' refusal to defend the Pennsylvania frontier ultimately cost them control of the state assembly in the mid-1760s. From then on, Ulster Irishmen, along with German settlers, had a stronger political voice in Pennsylvania.

The western frontier of Pennsylvania was especially attractive to members of Presbyterian Seceder and Covenanter sects, who felt that the mainstream Presbyterian Church was not strict enough. The stern church elders punished infractions, such as intoxication and other improper behaviors, and their mediation often prevented many disputes from going to court. Nonetheless, alcohol consumption was an integral part of the culture transplanted from Ireland; typically, the church elders started their meetings with a dram of whiskey.

In the late 1700s, western Pennsylvania's main business was agriculture, and the region was an exceedingly remote hinterland of Philadelphia and Baltimore. The farmers who cleared the land were initially limited to subsistence farming and producing enough to feed their own families. Gradually, they began to produce a surplus and barter for other goods. Wheat, corn, rye, hemp and flax were all important crops. Abundant water power ensured that sawmills and gristmills rapidly appeared; these were the first stirrings of the region's industrial future. The first United States census in 1790 reveals a dispersed rural population, and Pittsburgh, the largest town at the time, had only 376 residents; 19 percent of the region's populace was Irish.

A proximate cause of immigration to America around 1800, for both Protestants and Catholics, was the failed Rebellion of 1798 in Ireland. The Reverend Robert Steele fled County Derry due to his alleged involvement in the 1798 rebellion and joined his merchant brother, William, who was already located in Pittsburgh. Steele became a minister to Pittsburgh's early Presbyterian congregation. The Reverend Thomas Ledlie Birch came to Washington County, where he could minister to "a number of his old hearers and neighbors from Ireland." His cousin Joseph Ledlie, who may have been the primary organizer of the Society of United Irishmen in southern County Derry during the rebellion, was sent into exile and came to western Pennsylvania as well.

The Mellon family, later known for their banking prowess, exemplified this pattern of chain migration; in the span of two decades, by 1818, all the men in the family had migrated. William Findley, the future leader of backcountry democracy, sought out fellow Covenanters from County Antrim as he migrated westward through Pennsylvania. Letters home extolled the availability of cheap land, and sometimes early settlers willed their farms to relatives in Ireland. These new immigrants continued to transplant all the varieties of Presbyterianism from Ulster to western Pennsylvania, and the primary religious conflict was not between Catholics and Protestants but among Presbyterian sects. One early indicator of how the Irish dominated early settlement in western Pennsylvania is that over 50 percent of those applying for naturalization in the courts of Allegheny between 1798 and 1840 were Irish. Washington County showed similar results but with lower overall numbers of applicants. Quite a few applicants were former Revolutionary War soldiers seeking to collect their pensions.

The great difficulty in getting goods over the mountains contributed to the early transformation of the area into a manufacturing center. Iron smelting, tool making, nail and wire manufacturing, glass blowing and boat building became important and growing enterprises. The field of furniture making is but one example where Pittsburgh rapidly moved from producing inferior but serviceable goods to creating quality work that rivaled that of eastern manufacturers. Irish laborers were among those who constructed the National Road, which placed Pittsburgh on a commercial artery that ran from Cumberland, Maryland, to Vandalia, Illinois. Commenced in 1811, this was the first federal highway, and some suspect that the Irish immigrant laborers had help from leprechauns, who cursed the road so that it would forever remain under construction.

The War of 1812 made Pittsburgh an important supply depot for troops attempting to wrest Canada from England. Irish Presbyterian merchants and mill owners prospered, despite the fact that sometimes they had to sue the government for payment. Often left out of the conventional narratives is the fact that many Irish immigrants made a living as shopkeepers, even if they did not amass a fortune or leave a chain store to posterity. Peddling was the best way to enter this line of commerce because it required little capital investment in inventory and maintaining a storefront. Consequently, the "Diamond," or Market Square, of early Pittsburgh thronged with Irish and German peddlers hawking their wares. By 1850, the Irish dominated the peddling trade, accounting for over half of the city's peddlers, although only 2 percent of Irishmen chose to follow this trade in Pittsburgh.

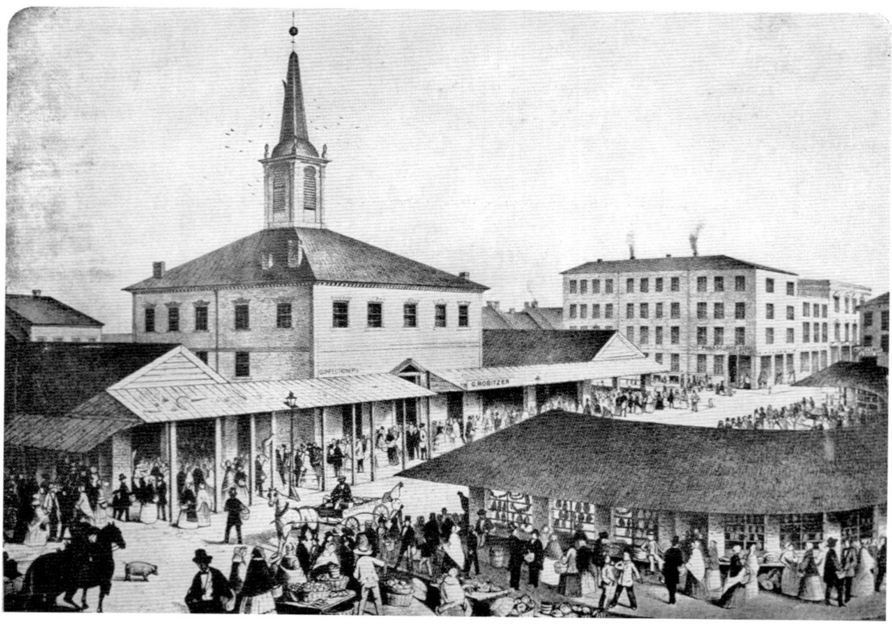

The marketplace in the Diamond. *Courtesy of the Catholic Historical Society.*

The skilled construction and metal trades provided early opportunities for Irishmen as well, in part because the city's German immigrants did not dominate these trades and because English-speaking Irishmen had a distinct advantage over German-speaking immigrants. Furthermore, a number of Irishmen had mastered metalworking skills, such as puddling, rolling and heating, by working in Scotland or England prior to their arrival in Pittsburgh. In the era before the invention of mass-produced steel and mechanization of the metalworking processes, skilled craftsmen fortunate enough to escape injury were the "aristocracy of labor." In their heyday, these craftsmen controlled the means of production, hired other workers and typically brought in thirteen to fifteen dollars a week at a time when common laborers were lucky to earn seventy-five cents a day.

This era also saw the beginnings of the first and oldest Catholic parish in the city of Pittsburgh: St. Patrick's, founded in 1808 at Eleventh Street. Although there were only about twenty Catholic families in the city at that time, Reverend William F.X. O'Brien was assigned to Pittsburgh to establish a parish. The church was built on a tight budget, and if a family wanted a pew, they had to pay for it themselves. As the population grew, however, an extension was added to the church in 1825. By 1827, it was apparent that a new church was needed. Father Charles McGuire, then pastor, called a meeting of local Catholics to plan for the construction of St. Paul's Cathedral. A steady flow of German and Irish immigrants fed the growth of the Catholic population in the early 1800s, but the city was, and in many ways still is, strongly influenced by its Presbyterian founders.

The Whiskey Rebellion

Allegheny County also was a rich farming area, and it produced a surplus of grain, which could not be shipped back over the mountains because of the expense. Whiskey was far more portable than grain, and the typical estimate was that one wagonload of whiskey replaced twelve of grain. Distilling grain into readily salable whiskey brought badly needed cash to a debtor region that still functioned as a barter economy in many places. The chain of events that led to the Whiskey Rebellion began when Alexander Hamilton, secretary of the treasury, put together an agreement between the states and the federal government in which this new national government would assume all the debts incurred by the states after the Revolutionary War. In return, the states agreed that the nation's capital city would be moved to the banks of the Potomac River between Virginia and Maryland.

Land sales were not sufficient to pay this federal debt, so Hamilton came up with the idea of imposing an excise tax on whiskey, which killed any profit by the farmers from the sale of an important cash crop. When the federal tax took effect in 1791, farmers began attacking tax collectors, particularly in Washington and Allegheny Counties. Other factors aggravated the high excise tax on whiskey that prompted the 1794 insurrection, including lack of protection from the Indians, lack of access to the Mississippi River, absentee landlords and a lack of federal courts, which necessitated trips to Philadelphia for trial. Since whiskey served as currency and many workers accepted it as payment instead of wages, the excise tax was an (arguably unconstitutional) income tax on poor laborers. Pennsylvania frontiersmen, long estranged from the colonial government in Philadelphia, saw little benefit in the new federal arraignment. Ulster Presbyterians had escaped English persecution in Ireland and fought the American War of Independence over "taxation without representation" only to be faced with a bold and unacceptable new tyranny. Taxing "the water of life" was simply a bad idea, although some, including frontier congressman William Findley, argued that Hamilton was not ignorant; he deliberately provoked conflict that would allow the federal government to assert its power to impose a tax that happened to favor large eastern distilleries.

Had western Pennsylvania been a prosperous region flush with hard currency, its residents would have objected to the new tax on principles alone, but there were economic and demographic factors underlying the Whiskey Rebellion. The good land had been quickly snatched up and consolidated by eastern speculators, and most established frontier families lost out in the race to acquire land that commenced in the 1770s. The result was an increase in the number of absentee landlords (including George Washington), who extracted rent but delegated management of their properties and could not be reached for complaint. The available good land went to the early, the fortunate or the unscrupulous, but thousands of people, often deceived by propaganda pamphlets, continued to pour into western Pennsylvania. New arrivals were disappointed to find not a homestead but backbreaking work clearing trees from the land already taken by speculators. Ulster Presbyterians who had fled rack-renting landlords in Ireland were not about to quietly acquiesce to the same exploitation in western Pennsylvania. The landless population surged as people continued to pour into the region. The poverty and squalid living conditions in and around Pittsburgh shocked well-off travelers from eastern cities, who expected some comfortable quarters after traversing the Allegheny Mountains.

The rebellion was a lengthy affair, lasting from 1791 to 1794, and it played out against the backdrop of the French Revolution. Educated upper-class men, in Pennsylvania and around the new country, feared the consequences of mob rule. Extremists had their own flag with six alternating red and white stripes that stood for the (hopefully) unified six counties of western Pennsylvania and northwestern Virginia. But it was apparent to more conservative members of the community that the issues extended beyond taxation and secession to the redistribution of wealth, particularly land. Pittsburgh, although ridiculously small, was viewed as "Sodom," an outpost of federalism, and there were calls by extremists to burn the city. Hugh Henry Brackenridge was a lawyer and satirist who led one of the moderate factions in western Pennsylvania that sought to avoid conflict with the federal government. He held a low opinion of uneducated frontiersmen, many of whom were from Ireland, who, in his opinion, could not be trusted to run civic affairs. In *Modern Chivalry*, Brackenridge's 1792 frontier satire, he described an electoral contest between an honest deacon and an ignorant Ulsterman: "When they looked on the one, they felt an inclination to promote him. But when again on the other hand, they saw two kegs which they knew to be replenished with a very cheering liquor, they seemed to be in favor of the other. But appetite prevailed, and they gave their vote in favor of the man with the two kegs." Moderates such as Findley and Brackenridge had trouble walking a middle ground, where they attempted to argue against both the tax and the need for federal intervention. If they appeared too sympathetic to the federal position, they risked being attacked themselves.

Residents of western Pennsylvania first threatened the excise tax collectors and then escalated their pressure as tax collectors were beaten or tarred and feathered. Tax collectors' houses were burned, and they faced eviction from their offices by apprehensive landlords. In 1794, federal marshals were assaulted when they attempted to serve writs for nonpayment of taxes, which were documents that summoned to Philadelphia any scofflaw who failed to pay the tax. In one case, William Miller was summoned from his farm in South Park to Philadelphia for trial and threatened with a ruinous fine. A group of local anti-tax forces came to his aid and chased off the marshal. In instances such as this, rounding up a sheriff's posse was a tricky proposition because it was difficult to raise a posse from the instigators or their sympathizers

An attack on tax inspector General Neville—which turned into a lengthy battle that ended with the burning of his home, Bower Hill—compelled

President George Washington to resort to a long-deferred military solution. Ultimately, the farmers were no match for the power of Washington, then in his first presidential term, who could not afford to lose this first test of the new government's power. The rebellion fizzled out, and its participants scattered long before an overwhelming force of nearly thirteen thousand federal troops reached the western Pennsylvania area. In the aftermath, respectable and property-owning citizens blamed the uprising on ruffians who had nothing to lose, and indeed, the Whiskey Rebellion could be readily viewed as an instance of overt class warfare.

This episode did have a lasting effect on the region; anti-federalist sentiments stemming from this period later contributed to the development of the Democratic Party and its stronghold in western Pennsylvania. After the rebellion, the area settled down to the business of becoming one of the most important manufacturing centers of the new nation. The rapid movement of settlers into the Ohio Valley created new markets, stimulated the growth of new industries and ensured the importance of Pittsburgh as a commercial center.

Frontier Music

One avenue of approaching Irish identity in the Pittsburgh region is to sidestep issues of religion and examine another central aspect of Irish culture: music. The people who arrived in the eighteenth century brought with them their music and instruments, especially fiddles and pipes. Dancing and music were important pastimes in frontier life, and the dances of the western Pennsylvania frontier were largely the same as those found in Ireland: jigs, reels, hornpipes and country dances with four facing four. The reel of the three and the reel of four (or the common reel), which would today be called "ceili dances," were transplanted from Ireland. These tunes were played as early as 1769, when Joseph Doddridge noted the popularity of three- and four-hand jigs and the "Irish trot," a round dance from the Ulster Plantation in which the women wound in and about their partners. Larger taverns had rooms for dancing and served Monongahela Rye, a frontier favorite.

The plantation of Scotsmen in the north of Ireland had both continued and redefined the long-established musical interaction between Scotland and Ireland while also sowing the seeds of an enduring sectarian conflict. The new Scots settlers brought jigs and weavers' ballads with them to Ireland, yet many of their dance tunes were similar to those enjoyed by the Irish. When the Ulster Irish Presbyterians immigrated to America, they brought their tunes and ballads with them as well. A *ceili*, or visit, was always a good occasion for music. On long, dark winter nights during the harvest time flax pullings and corn huskings or at weddings and wakes, the neighbors would gather for song and merriment. The sound of the fiddle and Irish dance tunes was ubiquitous on the frontier, and English travelers found the "boisterous, assertive, undisciplined and convivial culture of the region" to be akin to the "wild Irish in Ireland." This distinctive musical heritage gave Appalachian music its unique flavor. Francis O'Neil, the Irish music collector, noted in 1913, "The music of the fiddle has a wonderful hold on the affections of the people of West Virginia, Kentucky and Tennessee, many of whom are the descendants of Irish settlers of the 18th century." Many settlers lived in southwestern Pennsylvania before migrating south and west; it was easier to follow the valleys than cross the mountain ridges, so migrants within the mountains often moved north to south. Some of these settlers or their descendants eventually crossed the Mississippi River. Consequently, this dispersal of Irish Presbyterian culture led Colin Woodard to define a large swath of America as "Greater Appalachia," one of his eleven "nations" that constitute the United States and Canada.

Although the Presbyterian elders of Washington County officially warned against horse racing, balls and dances (because of the associated tendencies toward drunkenness and other sins), secular music itself was rarely condemned. Early Pittsburgh was home to a fiddler named "Crowder" who frequented the fairs on Grant's Hill, which was the edge of the early city. Hugh Henry Brackenridge wrote of Pittsburgh's popular races, "Dogs barked and bit, and horses trod on men's toes, and booths fell down on people's heads! There was Crowder with his fiddle and his votaries, making the dust fly with a four-handed or rather four-footed reel; and a little farther on was Dennis Loughy, the blind poet, like Homer; casting his pearls before swine, chanting his master-piece in a tone part nasal and part guttural."

Samuel P. Bayard's first published collection of Pennsylvania's traditional music, *Hill Country Tunes*, details the process of Irish influence on Pennsylvania traditional music. Bayard, a folklorist from Greene County, reported that in German-speaking areas of Pennsylvania he heard Irish and Scottish reels played on the radio by fiddlers with distinctly German names. Bayard attributed this crossover to eighteenth-century settlement patterns. Musicians, always keen to borrow a good riff or melody, continuously adapted and blended their music in western Pennsylvania. According to Kirby Miller, the result was "a blend of Ulster Scottish, native Irish and Anglo-American forms." Migration from Ulster to the western Pennsylvania frontier may have transplanted the religious animosities of the Ulster Plantation, but it also brought a complex, shared and evolving musical tradition that ultimately influenced a diverse family of musical genres that includes bluegrass and rock-and-roll, to name only two.

Donegal on the Allegheny (Armstrong County)

At the conclusion of the American Revolution, there were far more Irish Catholics in Pennsylvania than the standard narrative would lead us to imagine. In 1785, there were seven thousand Catholics in Pennsylvania, mostly Irish and German, according to Father John Carroll. West of the mountains, churches were scarce and priests overextended, although by the early 1800s, churches that no longer stand today had been built in Brownsville, Latrobe and Loretto. The oldest extant Catholic church building west of the Alleghenies is St. Patrick's—not in Pittsburgh but near Sugar Creek in Donegal Township, in today's Armstrong County.

At the end of the eighteenth century, a group of immigrants from Donegal, Ireland, arrived in Philadelphia on the ship *Eliza*. Moving inland, they crossed the Allegheny River and settled west of Buffalo Creek in 1798. Traveling priests visited the Buffalo Creek Mission until Father Sylvester Phelan took up residence. The church was completed, frontier style, by 1806, and the construction of this twenty-two-foot-wide structure was a community effort. Four men—Caspar Easley, Connell McCue, James Sheridan and Neil Sweeny—each took on the task of raising the money and manpower to build a particular wall, while Patrick McElroy was responsible for the roof. First they raised a few scarce dollars from their assigned districts. In 1805, they arrived on a designated day with a wall-building team. Oak trees were cut and skinned by hand, and to reduce the amount of cutting required, the windows were placed low in the walls. Despite the use of clay and straw to fill in gaps, the resulting structure was undoubtedly drafty. It was even more so because finishing the roof required waiting for nails, a scarce frontier commodity. The structure was finally completed in the fall of 1806 and served until 1847.

Although the congregation rapidly outgrew the log church, this first building would be pressed into service again. In 1872, the second St. Patrick's

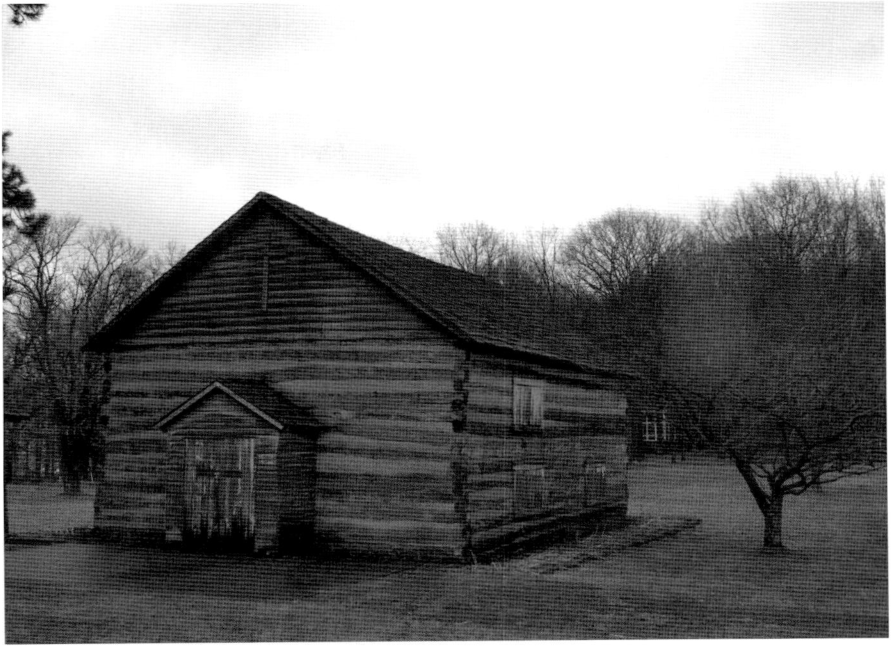

St. Patrick's Church, Sugar Creek. *Courtesy of Janis Ferrainolo.*

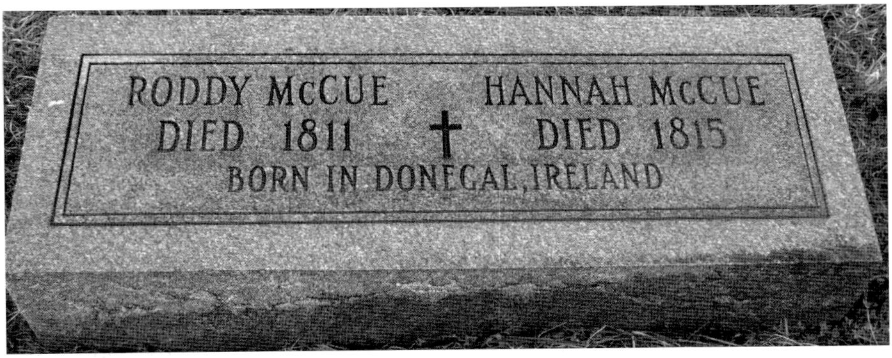

McCue headstone, St. Patrick's Church, Sugar Creek. *Courtesy of Janis Ferrainolo.*

Church burned in a possible arson. The original log church, which at that time was a schoolhouse, was used for four years until the replacement was completed. In 1926, after years of neglect, the log church was restored by the parish with assistance from local historians. This time, more nails were available. The restoration was fortuitous because lightning destroyed the third St. Patrick's Church in 1929, and the log church was again used by the parish. The sturdy log church endures, with its wooden benches and the restored cemetery nearby, as a reminder of an Irish community that arrived together and stayed together.

Part II

THE YOUNG CITY, 1820–1860

Many Irishmen built the Pennsylvania Canal, which, after its long traverse over the Allegheny Mountains, finally entered Pittsburgh at Eleventh Street, right by St. Patrick's Church. Large-scale construction of canals and railroads was a major cause for the Irish movement westward. Across the Monongahela River, they clustered in the Old Limerick neighborhood on the south side that is now Station Square. Pittsburgh historian Victor Walsh has calculated that by 1850, ten thousand Irish immigrants constituted 21.4 percent of the city's population of nearly fifty thousand people; similar demographic shifts were occurring across the Allegheny River in Allegheny City long before it was annexed and became the North Side of Pittsburgh. Many of these immigrants came from areas in Ireland that were relatively advanced economically—that is, industrializing counties with growing towns, larger farmsteads and lower rates of tenancy. Another analysis by Walsh found that 52 percent of the Irish workforce were unskilled, 30 percent were skilled or semi-skilled and 15 percent were white-collar workers. These figures are very different from those of other U.S. cities, such as Boston, where the Irish population was made up overwhelmingly of unskilled laborers.

Perhaps the best explanation of this phenomenon lies in the origins of Irish Pittsburgh in the years preceding the Civil War. Over 50 percent of Pittsburgh's Irish population in 1850 originated from Ulster, according to Walsh's analysis of surnames, which relied on British Parliamentary reports of name distributions in Ireland. While his method admittedly has flaws,

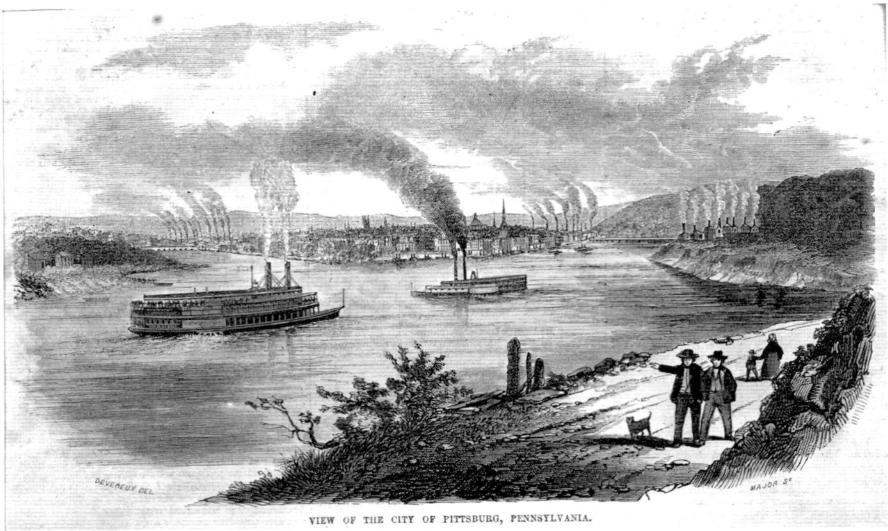

Pittsburgh from McKee's Rocks, 1853. *Courtesy of Carnegie Library of Pittsburgh, Oakland.*

there is no other way to examine region of origin because parish, census and immigration records in the United States simply note "Ireland" as their place of origin ("N. Ireland" appears in Pittsburgh census records beginning in 1930). In pre-famine Ireland, East Ulster was the sole industrializing region. The mechanization of spinning and linen production ended the cottage industries of weaving and spinning, and practitioners of these crafts were compelled to migrate within Ireland to the growing towns along the Lagan and Bann Valleys or seek work in England or America. In the western portions of Ulster, poor land and dense population drove the exodus.

In 1850, 20 percent of Irish Pittsburgh hailed from Leinster, where the port cities of Wicklow, Cork, Dublin and Dundalk connected the English market with its Irish hinterlands. Successful farmers in this region were reluctant to divide their land among increasing numbers of sons and tenants. In other parts of Leinster, the land was ideal for cattle raising, and the mostly Anglican landlords began to refuse to renew the leases of their Catholic tenants, creating another immediate reason for emigration. Surnames suggest that 15 percent of Irish antebellum Pittsburgh came from the province of Munster, another area of rich farmland that was cleared of Catholic tenants after the Napoleonic Wars. At this time, only 10 percent of Irish Pittsburgh originated from Connaught, "a world sealed off from the outside by impassable moors and mountains…beyond the orbit of a modernizing Anglo-Irish market economy and culture," according to Walsh. As we shall see, however, a few Connaughtmen can cause a heap of trouble.

Middle-class, or "lace curtain," Irish served in church leadership and began making inroads into politics. On the edge of downtown (now Grant Street), they formed a prosperous community around St. Paul's Cathedral, while the poorer groups and single men who were unskilled day laborers settled into the Hill District. Unemployment was high among Hill District men, and it was not until 1853 that the Irish of the Hill were able to raise the money for St. Bridget's Church, a simple red brick structure. Others moved into the Strip District, living in proximity to their work in the iron and glass industries, and another group of Irish industrial workers resided along Woods Run in Allegheny City.

Western Pennsylvania's burgeoning Catholic population suffered from a lack of clergy. The situation began to change when, in December 1843, Pittsburgh's first bishop, Michael O'Connor, arrived with money from Germany. However, the impoverished people of Ireland could only afford to send their sons and daughters; eight seminarians from Maynooth and seven sisters from the recently founded Order of Our Lady of Mercy in Dublin committed themselves to building a community in a country unknown to them. The Pittsburgh foundress of the Sisters of Mercy was Mother Francis Xavier Warde.

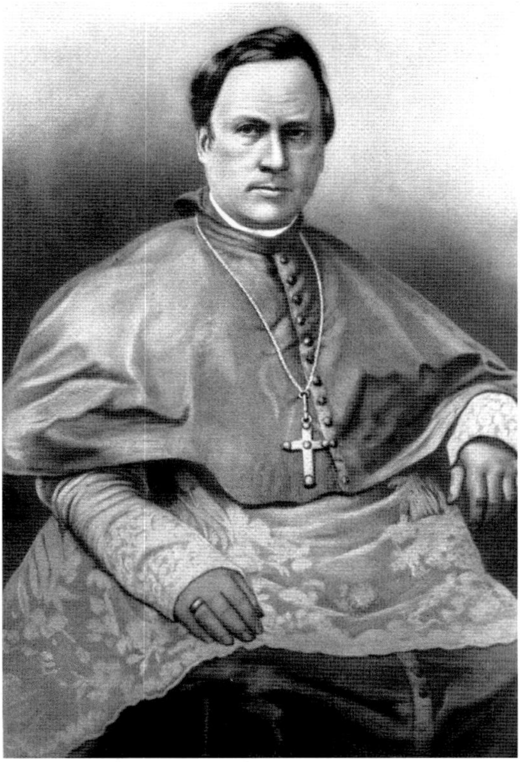

Bishop O'Connor. *Courtesy of the Catholic Historical Society.*

Historians refer to this stage of urban development as the era of "the walking city," when everyone, regardless of wealth or status, lived in proximity to the wharfs, mills, stores, etc. that provided employment. Poor people had to either pay

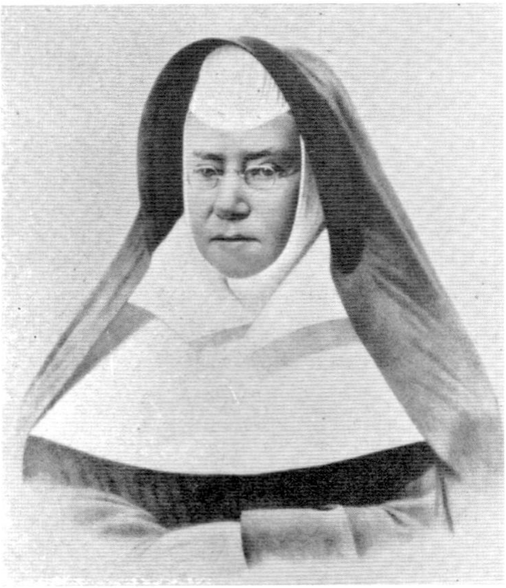

Left: Mother Francis Xavier Warde. *Courtesy of the Catholic Historical Society.*

Below: Mercy Hospital in 1848. *From* "Flem's" Views of Old Pittsburgh.

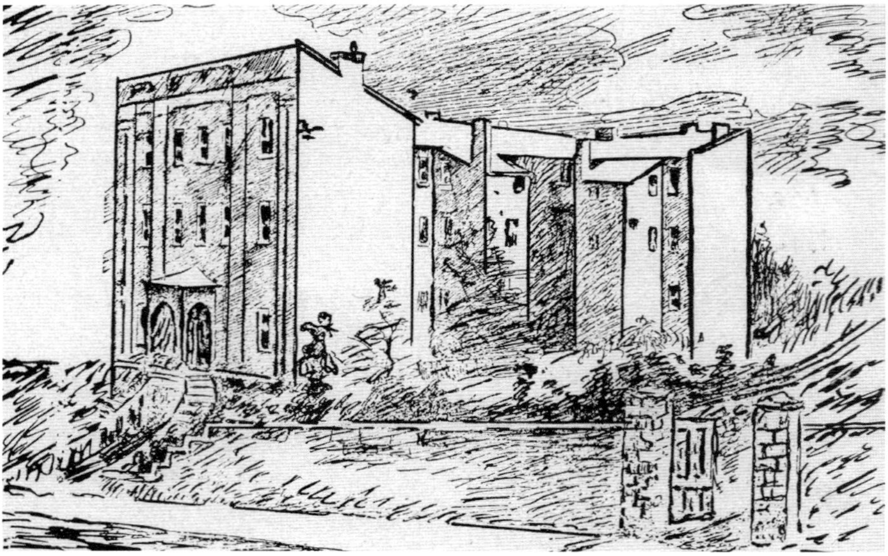

high rent for cramped quarters near workplaces or walk farther. Rich people could afford large houses downtown, but they could not isolate themselves from the rest of the city until the advent of railroads and streetcars. Generally speaking, at this stage in the history of the development of cities, much of the infrastructure that we take for granted today did not exist or was planned haphazardly. Building, fire and health codes did not exist. Garbage was not picked up, and human waste was allowed to flow into the same rivers that everyone drank from. Consequently, outbreaks of fire and disease were both common and devastating to all Pittsburghers. Just as the Great Chicago Fire of 1870 was attributed to "Mrs. O'Leary's cow" knocking over a lantern, the Great Fire of Pittsburgh in 1845 has been attributed to Ann Brooks, an Irish washerwoman who left a fire for heating water unattended on a windy day.

On the other hand, an outbreak of smallpox later in 1845 led to a powerful contribution to Pittsburgh by its Irish community: the establishment of Mercy Hospital, despite the limited resources available to the Sisters of Mercy. At the time, the smallpox ward was a repurposed coal shed, and public support for a hospital was limited. The Sisters of Mercy converted part of the former theater that was their residence into a temporary hospital. With the support of Bishop O'Connor and local pastors, they raised funds for a permanent hospital, which opened in 1848.

Within Pittsburgh, Irish settlement crept away from downtown into the Strip District and Lawrenceville. In August 1854, a machine shop next to St. Patrick's caught fire, which spread to the church and burned it to the ground. A new church would be built at Fourteenth Street, which eventually was sold to the Pennsylvania Railroad Company. Another plot of ground at Seventeenth Street was purchased, and the third St. Patrick's Church was built, including catacombs under the church and courtyard. While never the largest church in Pittsburgh, St. Patrick's Church has always remained a symbolic center of Irish Pittsburgh, even as it moved repeatedly.

Dousing Debauchery in "Old Galway" (Near Fifth and Liberty)

One early incident that illustrates the colorful life of the "walking city" is the "Great Brothel Dousing," a prank or frolic instigated by firefighters at the expense of the less respectable class in Pittsburgh. At around ten o'clock in the evening on Wednesday, June 1, 1842, volunteer firefighters converged at Blind Sam's, a house of ill repute at Grant Street and Fourth Avenue that was run by a German fiddler. Well aware that the building was not on fire, firefighters nonetheless directed their hoses at the front windows, forcing all and sundry to flee in various states of undress. The next night, firefighters decided to "clean up" the infamous Crow's Nest at Wood Street and Virgin

Alley. Again directing streams of water through the front windows, they gave "the smiling faces of Mrs. Murphy and Hannah Johnson" a "refreshing shower." According to the *Pittsburgh Morning Chronicle*:

> *The door was then closed, and the whole of the nest, of all colors, fledged and unfledged, drunk and sober, took a flight the back way. The retreating squad was headed by a Maria Ramsey, in the ranks were old Mother Murphy, Hannah Reams, and Hannah Johnson, or Williams, while Henry Johnson, the husband of the last named, commonly known as the* Irish Nagur, *(accompanied by a few "nice young men;") brought up the rear! The besieged thus effected a retreat with* flying colors. [emphasis in original]

This sort of community action against brothels was not a new development in early America, but it now reflected problems in a rapidly expanding urban area that was seeing an influx of foreigners, especially Irish, Germans and Africans. Transient laborers and the newly arrived working poor were seen as carriers of vice and immorality. However, because vice was commonly perceived as a victimless crime, as opposed to robbery or murder, enforcement of laws against prostitution, chronic drunkenness and fighting was generally ineffective. There was no regular police force, only the night watch, which had been reduced from twenty-two to eleven men to cut costs. In antebellum Pittsburgh, the Mayoral Election Day in early January was an annual outbreak of vigilante activity against moral depravity that featured flaming tar barrels and other incendiary devices. The absence of a professional and effective police force partly explains why volunteer firefighters were able to take matters into their own hands. Newspaper descriptions of brothel house and grogshop incidents were sure to note the ethnicities of the ne'er-do-wells involved while omitting the identities of the "nice young men" from respectable families. Disturbances earlier in the year at the Crow's Nest led to court testimony of "scenes of amalgamation that would have disgraced a slave plantation." Historians may dispute the degree and nature of tendencies to equate the Irish with Africans, but the *Manufacturer* gleefully told its readers that the "purifiers" of Hanna Murphy's establishment watched "Molly Murphy the 'Irish Nigger,' the 'Bay Nigger,' and every other kind of niggers fly from the premises in quick time." The dousing was calculated to appeal to widespread nostalgia among the majority population for a homogenous community that never was. Simply put, the firefighters were bullies who sought to enhance their reputation and political power at the expense of people who could not fight back.

To a large extent, the lower-class immigrants were also victims of a complex political struggle between the night watch and volunteer firefighters that centered on mayoral appointment power and other political "spoils" that went to the victor of each year's mayoral election. Fire companies were not all created equal, and they occupied the middle and lower rungs of a social hierarchy that privileged membership in the Freemasons, the Bible Society and the Library Society. Some hose companies were run by the sons of elite families and had up-to-date equipment, but other companies were basically youth gangs with barely functioning water pumps. Yet the civil-minded volunteers claimed superiority to "mere hirelings" and strongly resisted attempts to establish tax-funded professional services. In many incidents, watchmen and firefighters were blamed for the very riots and fires they were supposed to control. The best that can be said is that the responses of both watchmen and firefighters were lackluster, slow or nonexistent when it suited their political situation.

An example of this unprofessional emergency response occurred during the June 4, 1842 culmination of this wave of vigilante activity. A mob seeking to punish a Mrs. Turney, who kept a "disorderly" house in the Fifth Ward, started a fire that destroyed seventeen buildings and left twenty-two "poor but honest" families homeless. Volunteers themselves appear to have set the fire, and only a few men from the Niagara Company attempted to fight the rapidly spreading blaze. The notorious Crow's Nest and its denizens were perennial features in the news until it was burned down by young rowdies on April 27, 1850. The police made no attempt to stop the "boys" who battled for control of the building and repeatedly failed in their attempts to set fire to the building before finally succeeding. No word on the whereabouts of the fire companies on that night.

The "brothel dousing" incidents at Blind Sam's and the Crow's Nest were examples of an attempt to use a traditional communal organization, albeit a less prestigious one, for a new purpose. Blaming new arrivals for social decline was a common theme, but attacks on highly visible representations of vice were considered more acceptable than attacking grocers or washerwomen.

Rioting on the Railroads

As rail transportation superseded canals and the railroads began to push west of Pittsburgh, western Pennsylvania saw the continuation of a long-running feud that had plagued canal-building enterprises from Maryland all the way to Indiana, notoriously so in the 1830s. A "war" between railroad worker gangs (in all senses of the term) broke out on the Pittsburgh and Steubenville Line. The rival worker factions were commonly referred to in contemporary accounts as "Corkonians" (mostly from County Cork in the Province of Munster) and "Fardowns" (from the Province of Connaught). Contractors and work bosses knew that they had to hire only one faction for any particular work project along the line. While this precaution didn't guarantee peace, it often worked. Corkonians and Fardowns built the rail line to Pittsburgh without any newsworthy incidents—but it must be noted that brawls and murders in distant work camps generally went unreported. To further complicate construction, villages and shantytowns along railroad right of ways were frequently allied with one of the factions.

The Cross Creek "war" began in February 1852 when a workforce of Fardowns on the Pittsburgh and Steubenville Line was preparing to build a bridge at Cross Creek, near the Virginia panhandle. When a mill owner objected, saying that he had not given permission, his workers (presumably Corkonians or their allies) confronted the Fardowns and drove them away. The Fardowns responded by returning in greater numbers. They drove the Corkonians "back on the line to section 25," according to the *Steubenville Herald*, and "supposing themselves 'monarchs of the soil,' entered farmhouses, and demanded what they wished to satisfy hunger and comfort; enforcing the same by presenting pistols at the heads of men and women." Searching for Corkonians, the Fardowns swore vengeance against anybody hiding one as they plundered the countryside.

In the vicinity of Pittsburgh, hundreds of Corkonians, many of them fully armed, were determined to drive the Fardowns off the line. They marched into Pittsburgh with the intent of journeying to Cross Creek to assist their fellows. Conflicting accounts suggest that few of them were able to get there, however, because the steamship captains refused to take them. Some of the belligerent Corkonians were arrested in Pittsburgh as the authorities tried to control the situation. In any event, it seems they would have arrived at Cross Creek too late to affect the outcome of the conflict.

As Fardowns terrorized the Cross Creek populace, farmer Adam Reed was confronted with a drawn pistol. He responded by knocking his attacker flat with a well-placed punch and ran to Steubenville to raise the alarm. Emerging from Steubenville, a sheriff's posse encountered about twenty farmers commanded by a George McCullogh. Armed with rifles, these outraged farmers had somehow managed to take five hundred Fardown prisoners by surrounding them and compelling them to give up their weapons, and a dozen or so ringleaders were jailed.

Events in Pittsburgh were watched with interest in faraway places like Troy, New York, where improvements on the Erie Canal were about to begin and mayhem was anticipated. This era of feuding was drawing to a close, however, even though large-scale hostilities later broke out in February 1857 at the Bergen Tunnel in New Jersey. As historian Malcolm Campbell has noted, "Gradually, inevitably, the lived experience of immigration and the newcomers' standing as a minority community in their new societies operated to diminish old localisms and forge an Irish national identity." The railroad war over Cross Creek represented the end of an era, partly because geographic distinctions were less important to the new generation of American-born Irish and partly because of an ongoing need to stand together against the rising nativist hostilities of the pre–Civil War decade.

Contemporary commentary on these events by outsiders and/or reporters from far away was often biased and misleading. Reports frequently bemoaned the effects of "demon rum" and insisted the solution was worksite prohibition on alcohol. The perspective of the "lace curtain Irish" is demonstrated in a reaction to the Cross Creek "war" that was published on February 21, 1852, in the *Irish American*:

> *In the name of the LORD, what can these unhappy men mean? In the name of poor Ireland, why do our misguided fellow countrymen behave so savagely in their adopted country…yield to brutal instincts, and, thus, disgrace their native country and race?…The* causes *of these quarrels proceed from competition among contractors;…and in the wholesale use of poisoned liquors at the* shanties.

In this excerpt, we see provincial identification weakening in favor of identification as "fellow countrymen," coupled with a tension within the upper classes of Irish immigrants—identifying with the dominant views of their adopted land while retaining the need to uphold their native country. Distant writers were apparently not aware that when railroads did prohibit alcohol at the worksite, the Irish simply drank and fought at night, and it can be imagined that no increase in productivity was seen. Furthermore, the financing of railroads was always shaky, and contractors were known to encourage fighting when they knew they could not pay their men because a good riot was an excuse to skip payday—and skip town if necessary. More problematic is an understandable assumption, perpetuated by many

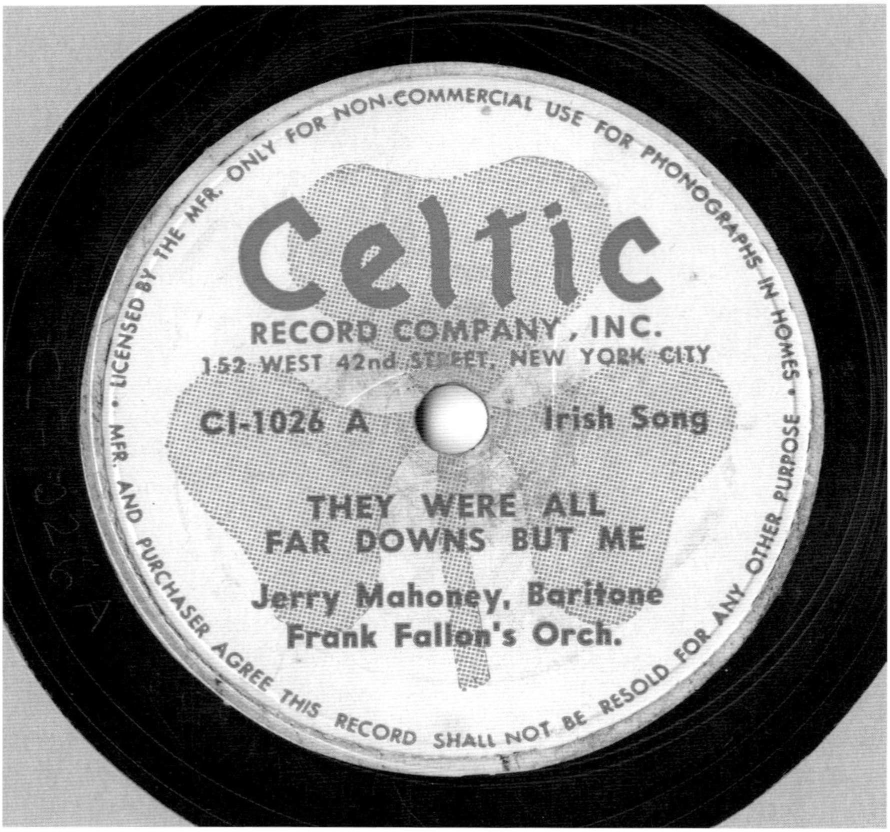

Jerry Mahoney's 1950s song "They Were All Far Downs but Me." *Courtesy of Ted McGraw.*

American historians, that these feuds had a religious aspect. They did not; this conflict between Catholic immigrants was purely economic, and Protestants from the northern province of Ulster were not a faction in the railroad wars. This inaccurate notion of the Fardowns was even committed to vinyl in the 1950s in a song by Jerry Mahoney, "They Were All Far Downs but Me," with its references to "The Battle of the Boyne" and so forth.

Finally, the term "Fardowns" deserves a bit of explanation because reporters and subsequent historians frequently gave explanations that were dubious or flat-out wrong. Fardown is not the name of any province or county in Ireland. The term may have two or more independent origins and meanings, but we are concerned here with the meaning found in the specific context of the railroad wars in antebellum America. A good place to start would be the diary of Andrew Leary O'Brien, an ex-seminarian who kept a journal when working for the railroad near Lancaster, Pennsylvania. A Cork immigrant himself who held an aloof view of his rough and illiterate co-workers, O'Brien tells us, "One contract they were all Fardowns (that is from the lower counties of Ireland). The next contract was worked by Corconians [*sic*], that is people from County Cork & the adjoining counties." At first glance, checking this explanation against a map makes no sense because you can't get any farther south than Cork without walking on water; however, the south of Ireland, particularly the province of Munster, is mountainous, and "lower" can be read as a term describing elevation. Furthermore, we should bear in mind that many early Irish maps were drawn upside down before mapmaking was standardized and that before the compass reached Europe in the Middle Ages, orienting a map actually required the reader to physically face Jerusalem! Another credible contemporary source would be a denunciation of secret societies in 1842 by New York's archbishop John Hughes that condemned "disturbances on public works which are spoken of in the newspapers as between 'Corkonians and Connaughtmen—farups and fardowns.'" The term "Fardown" was a mystery to many newspapermen as well; the *New York Morning Herald* even solicited reader explanations and concluded, "The people of the south of Ireland apply that term [Fardownian] to those in the north of Ireland; and they love each other as Satan loves holy water."

Hibernians Arise in Pennsylvania

The origins of railroad factions can be connected or traced to secret societies in Ireland. Accents, dress and connections to specific families or villages would often be enough to establish whether a stranger was friend or foe. However, background checks take time, and passwords communicating membership in a secret society were common shorthand for signaling identity. Being secretive by nature, secret societies have been problematic for historians to investigate even when society members were literate because keeping meeting minutes and memos would have been a decidedly unsecure practice. Nonetheless, secrets were exposed following a militia raid on the shanties of Irish canal workers who had been warring against German laborers in 1839, and Fardown signs and passwords were subsequently published in the *Daily Cleveland Herald*:

The following are the pass-words and countersigns of the Connaughtmen…
Q. The winter is favorable.
A. So is friendship increasing
Q. True Connaughtmen is valiant [sic]
A. Yes, and never will be defeated
Quarreling Words
Q. That Connaughtmen may be steady
A. And they will be respected.
Pass Words
Q. That all Connaughtmen may be nice.
A. Yes, without they may meet their enemies.

These cryptic exchanges are examples of the traditional method of signaling membership in Irish peasant secret societies. The Protestant "Peep o' Day Boys" and the Catholic "Defenders" had long resorted to tactics and methods that were undeniably terroristic, but their actions could not rightly be called "ethnic cleansing" because their feuding was a religious conflict. The British government was repeatedly compelled to ban the Orange order secret societies that emerged in the 1790s. Their systemic warfare against Catholics did not simply make parts of Ulster ungovernable; on occasion, these Protestant secret societies plotted against the Crown itself. Many Catholic secret societies thrived as well, sometimes associated with the better-known Defenders, Whiteboys and Ribbon Men, sometimes independently. The connection between American and Irish secret societies was not a one-way flow, as is evident in the following passwords used by Ribbon Men, uncovered in 1833 in Ireland:

Q. How long is your stick?
A. Long enough to reach my enemies
Q. To what trunk does the wood belong?
A. To a French trunk that blooms in America and whose leaves shall shelter the sons of Erin

The wrong answer in the wrong place could mean violent death not only in Ireland but in Pennsylvania as well; this was not "Raccoon Lodge" tomfoolery. As Andrew O'Brien noted of the Corkonian-Fardown feud in his journal, "So deadly was the character of their enmity towards each other, that one of a different party even passing by the other party would be run down like a rabbit by a pack of bloodhounds, & murdered on the spot he was overtaken on." It appears that secret societies functioned not only on the American railways but also at the ports of arrival for Irish immigrants, who rarely arrived without some plan for employment and whose passage was frequently paid for by friends or family in America. The secret societies functioned as far-reaching networks for employment and self-defense that lacked central authority.

There were numerous Irish secret societies in the United States and Canada in the early 1800s, and the words "Hibernian" and "Shamrock" were frequently used by both Catholics and Protestants, so they cannot be used to reliably trace religious affiliations; however, the advent of the Ancient Order of Hibernians (AOH) in America is less murky. On St. Patrick's Day 1836, members of the Hibernian Benevolent Society from Pennsylvania's Schuylkill County met with New York members of the St. Patrick's Fraternal Society. An American branch of the Ancient Order of Hibernians developed from this meeting, with the first chapters in Pennsylvania and New York. The earliest AOH division in Pittsburgh was formed in the late 1840s, and Daniel Dougherty was the first Allegheny County delegate. Originally restricted to Irish-born Catholic men, membership in the AOH was secret, and meeting minute books used numbers instead of names. This early organization was different from the highly visible AOH that had emerged by 1900.

The AOH motto of "Friendship, Unity, and Christian Charity" is almost identical to that of the earlier Defenders and suggests a continuity of purpose extending back to 1565. American Hibernians were chartered by a parent organization of the same name that was closely aligned with the Ribbon Men of Ireland. Furthermore, the list of signers of the original charter from Ireland also notes the counties of the signers—Antrim, Cavan, Fermanagh, Leitrim, Longford, Mayo, Meath, Moneghan, Sligo and Tyrone, a wide geographical dispersion—and there is little evidence of old-country regionalism in the American branch of the AOH. The American experience slowly but surely led to a notion of Irish—as opposed to provincial—identity, and it should be noted that this forging of national identity in Pittsburgh was not unique to the Irish. It must be emphasized again that there are rarely simple narratives and that Irish nationalism in both the United States and Ireland has had both Catholic and Protestant adherents throughout its long history.

Lest the reader think the author is biased in his approach to Irish secret societies, it must be pointed out that the Orange orders of nineteenth-century western Pennsylvania are also obscure. Victor Walsh has noted the existence of local lodges, such as the Sons of Joshua in Lawrenceville or Lodge No. 78 in Southside, but little is known about them. Clashes between

Orangemen and Catholics on July 12 and March 17 were frequent and bloody in Pittsburgh but did not approach the scale of mayhem found in New York City in the 1870s. Orange orders were far more successful and long lasting in Canada, and a simple point might explain this: for all the nativists' fears that Irish Catholics served a "foreign prince"—the pope—Irish Protestants who upheld union with England essentially proclaimed their loyalty to the Crown of England, a profoundly un-American ideal.

The Bishop and the Bigot

Today it is difficult to imagine the hatred directed against Irish Catholics in the nineteenth century, which strongly resembles twenty-first-century hate directed at Islam and its adherents in many places in the United States. This connection between past and present was made explicitly clear on March 6, 2012, when Pittsburgh City Council voted unanimously to condemn a proposed state anti-Sharia law, HB2029. Councilman Bill Peduto compared it to "hate legislation" against Pittsburgh Catholics 150 years ago. Peduto added, "The Catholic Bishop was actually imprisoned, and the cathedral was burnt down…This is the exact type of thing we need to be fighting." While Peduto captured the spirit of the era correctly, he got his facts wrong: although a bishop was indeed arrested, tried and fined, no church was ever riotously burned in Pittsburgh. This was a dangerous era for Pittsburgh's Irish community that should be examined closely.

The occurrence of riots directed against Irish Catholics precedes 1847 and does not match the oft-taught narrative of famine-induced immigration. One of the worst outbreaks of anti-Catholic violence in America occurred in Pennsylvania. Events turned deadly in the Kensington area of Philadelphia in May 1844, when riots, fires, looting and gun battles broke out. When the mob set out to burn down St. Michael's Church on the afternoon of the eighth, the military made no serious attempt to stop them. As the church and its rectory burned, along with nearby factories and homes, the looting and dancing mob prevented several fire companies from approaching the fires. Ultimately, two hundred Irish Catholic families were left homeless, dozens were killed in fires and fighting and hundreds of thousands of dollars in property damage (millions today) occurred. All public buildings associated with Kensington's Irish Catholic community were destroyed, including schools, nunneries, the Hibernian Hose Company and the 260-foot-long Nanny Goat Market, which was the center of Irish life and trade in Kensington. Pittsburgh's Irish Catholics, along with responsible civic leaders, feared a repeat in their own city when a few local firebrands persisted in their attempts to incite a "Philadelphia riot."

As tensions mounted in Pittsburgh, Bishop O'Connor prepared for mayhem while seeking to avert it. Addressing St. Paul's congregation on Sunday, May 12, 1844, he proclaimed, "Stir neither hand nor foot; but if they attempt to fire your asylum or your church, defend them, and I will head you." While Philadelphia was experiencing yet another round of rioting in July 1844, Orangemen planned to parade through Pittsburgh on July 12, the time for commemorating Protestant William of Orange's military victory in Ireland. They cancelled the march, however, and assembled outside the city limits instead, thus avoiding direct provocation of Pittsburgh's Irish Catholic community.

This is not to say that there were no local consequences to sectarian conflict at the time—there are more subtle ways to destroy churches than burning them. One victim was the Chapel of the Nativity, a repurposed Methodist building that was dedicated by Bishop O'Connor on June 30, 1844, and intended to serve Pittsburgh's black Catholic population. The success of the chapel prompted allegations that Father Wilson was actually proslavery and that the chapel was a devious plot to bring blacks together so that they could be sold into southern slavery. The misinformation campaign succeeded, and the Chapel of the Nativity lasted only a year, as the church was emptied of its intended flock. For some, spreading malicious rumors was sufficient, but others in Pittsburgh had a taste for rioting.

The most notable Pittsburgh troublemakers of the era were John Barker, John Sharp and Hugh Kirkland. Their attempts at rabblerousing attracted audiences and repeatedly blocked Market Street and the Canal Bridge on Penn Street. From 1845 to 1849, Barker directed a steady stream of vitriol, insulting Bishop O'Connor as "Mickey" and Irish Catholics as "Mickies." To their credit, most Pittsburghers were not aroused to mob action, as the *Pittsburgh Post* noted on October 2, 1847:

> *All praise is due to our Irish and Catholic Fellow-citizens for their forbearance and tolerance towards the little faction that nightly hold meetings in the marketplace, and whose object evidently is to excite a "Philadelphia Riot." The friends of order and decency are sometimes attracted to these meetings; but in no case have the incendiary blackguards been interfered with…We are glad that they are such fools to hold their meetings in the*

> *market places, and on market evenings. It is well that the people from the country should know something about them.*

Yet Barker was persistent, offensive and undeterred by ridicule. His soapbox harangues continued, filled with vulgarity and lewd gestures, and finally Mayor John Herron had enough. Some accounts suggest that the last straw was an attempt at inciting a riot in front of St. Paul's Cathedral or St. Patrick's Church, but this remains unclear. What is known is that Barker, Sharp and Kirkland were arrested, tried and convicted on three counts: obstructing Main Street, obstructing Market Street and using "indecent, lewd, and immoral language, calculated to deprave the morals of the community." On November 7, 1849, a jury found the defendants guilty on all three counts. Barker was fined $250 and sentenced to a year in jail. During his jail term, however, Barker ran for the office of mayor, as he had many supporters and defenders, including the *Presbyterian Advocate*. He won the January 1850 municipal elections, and a triumphant mob forced his release from the county jail and carried him through the streets to the mayor's office. The mayor-elect returned to jail, awaiting a governor's pardon before taking office. Thus began a particularly dangerous chapter in the history of Irish Pittsburgh.

Once Barker was mayor, the shoe was on the other foot, so to speak. In August, when court was not in session, he had Bishop O'Connor arrested—ostensibly due to a sewage problem at the recently founded Mercy Hospital. "Judge" Barker personally tried the case and, despite his lack of judicial authority or evidence, found Bishop O'Connor guilty, with no opportunity to appeal. The bishop paid a twenty-dollar fine to avoid a jail sentence. Barker's election and continued street preaching emboldened militant nativists to petty thievery, cross burnings and window breaking. Threats of arson to Catholic buildings were made, and priests were harassed on the streets. Consequently, many priests put aside their clerical outfits, and guards were stationed around churches. The German parishioners of St. Philomena began building a high wall around their school and church. In a letter to the Paris Mission Society, O'Connor described his predicament:

> *What I fear is that these things will end in a riot. I am sure that that is what they desire and what they try to bring about. Up to the present time with the help of God we have succeeded in maintaining tranquility. For some weeks they have come every Sunday afternoon to give their discourses near the windows of the seminary. They are accompanied by a crowd of desperate men who have no religion or morals and who*

> *wish for nothing more than an excuse to attack us. They have the hope that Catholics will attack them. It is the Mayor himself who preached on these occasions. Since he is the one who names the members of the police you can understand what our security is. Last Sunday a group of German women attacked him by throwing stones. It will be necessary to prevent a repetition of this scene, otherwise we will have a repetition of the bloody riots of Philadelphia of 1844.*

Clearly, O'Connor sought to avert violence, which meant that both sides had to be restrained, but the phrase "you can understand what our security is" can be read two ways here: there was no security, or their "security" was extralegal and the "understanding" is that one or more secret societies were pledged to defend pulpit and prelate. Some protective organization, whether ad hoc or traditional, was indubitably in place, most likely an early version of the Ancient Order of Hibernians. The houses of God were watched and protected in ways that houses of ill repute were not. The greatest service of these clandestine protective groups to Irish Pittsburgh was their long nightly vigils in all weather, unrecorded perhaps but not unappreciated.

Protestants, too, had their secret societies, and the most famous from this era, aside from Freemasons, was the Know-Nothings, so named because when questioned about their activities they replied, "I know nothing." They were not a political party; instead, they pledged their support to any candidate with a clear anti-immigrant and anti-Catholic agenda and particularly to members of the Nativist Party. In Pittsburgh, the most dangerous secret society may have been the Protestant Association, which was purportedly exposed by an anonymous figure identifying himself only as "a Liberty St. Merchant" in a very interesting and inflammatory (in every sense of the word) letter to Bishop O'Connor on December 9, 1850. The mysterious figure concluded his conspiracy exposé thusly:

> *A few days ago in conversation with some of the members, on the progress of their constitution, after having enjoined* secrecy [emphasis in original] *upon me, related as follows…"You know the elections for mayor comes on shortly but* [take] *my word for it, it will not pass without carrying with it, the Popish Churches, convents, and Hospital. The plan has been laid. Theo. Southerland will be our leader—he lives in coal lane, and understands all about it. The plan of the same has been laid down on paper. There are a great many stables up there which are pretty well filled with hay. The Catholics have carried on long*

> *enough. The day for revenge is at hand." Such sir, is in substance the conversation I had, and my intention of writing you this letter is not to put the Catholics on alert, but the proper authorities, for I never want to witness again the scenes of May, 1844 in Philadelphia.*

Thus alerted, Bishop O'Connor ordered that buildings be guarded continuously, and it appears that would-be arsonists were discouraged. The conclusion of the letter suggests that the author was present in Philadelphia six years prior, but it is also possible that the letter was disinformation, written with the intent of provoking a Catholic overreaction, thereby creating a pretext for rioting. The hinted-at election day mayhem, a Pittsburgh tradition alluded to earlier, did not occur. Barker lost his bid for reelection (which was annual back then), and rabid Catholic baiting fell into disfavor. Several further election bids failed, and Barker was decapitated by a train in 1862. Lack of Protestant enthusiasm for Barker and his ilk did not mean that controversy faded; it only became less militant.

Even the city's plans to lower Grant Street were snarled in the sectarian conflict of the time. Today, Grant Street is a slight incline and Grant's Hill is all but unnoticeable, but "the hump" was a serious obstacle to commerce in early Pittsburgh. In the 1830s, plans were laid to regrade the streets. The first stage of the process did not threaten St. Paul's Cathedral at the intersection of Fifth Avenue and Grant Street, but in June 1847, the editor of the *Pittsburgh Catholic* strenuously objected to the second regrading: "We admit that in the legality of the thing the course of the Philadelphia mobs and the intended action differ widely, but as long as we have one breath to draw we shall ever denounce the injustice of the one and the other as perfectly on a par." After the streets were lowered, St. Paul's Cathedral was precariously perched and required the construction of access stairs and retaining walls to secure its foundation. A successful suit against the city led to an award of $4,000—far short of the cost of rebuilding. For three years, the cathedral was still used for worship until it was realized that they must salvage the cathedral and rebuild. Before the salvaging was completed, however, St. Paul's Cathedral burned in a midday fire on May 6, 1851.

This was a very delicate moment. Some accounts claimed that the roof of the cathedral caught fire by sparks from the bishop's chimney next door, but the *Pittsburgh Catholic* disputed these claims. O'Connor conducted his own investigation, and in a private letter years later to the editor of the *Morning Post*, he expressed his personal conviction that the fire was arson. In any event, if there ever was conclusive proof, it was withheld. Bishop

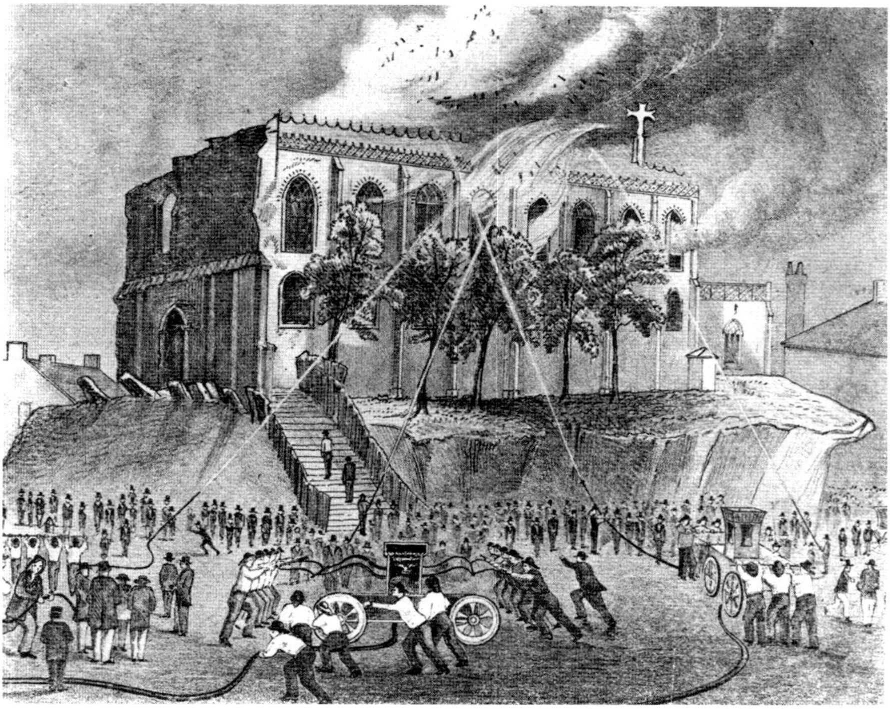

Above: St. Paul's Cathedral burns. *From* "Flem's" Views of Old Pittsburgh.

Right: The second St. Paul's Cathedral. *From* "Flem's" Views of Old Pittsburgh.

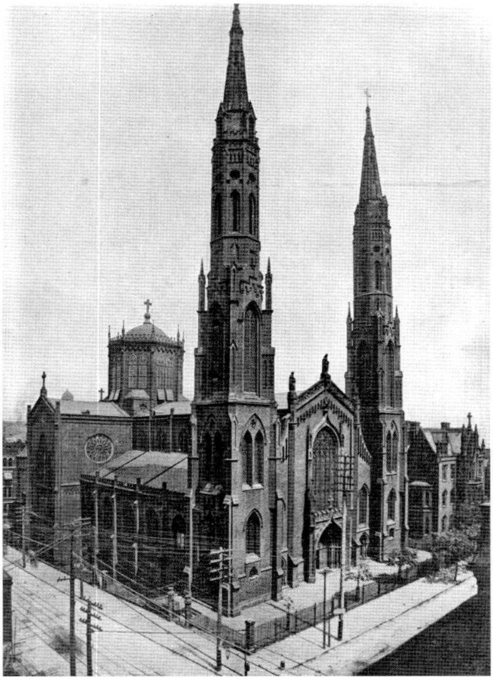

O'Connor declined to publicly state that the fire was arson, and this approach undoubtedly prevented an escalation of tensions within the city. The second St. Paul's Cathedral, a few blocks away at Fifth Avenue and Grant Street, was dedicated by Archbishop John Hughes on June 24, 1855. And no, this church did not burn as well—the site was later sold to Henry Clay Frick for his Union Trust Building, and a temple of Mammon replaced a house of God.

Ultimately, the biggest event of this era in Pittsburgh was what *didn't* happen: wide-scale rioting directed at the Irish people and their new institutions of learning, commerce, social life, healthcare and religion. It is

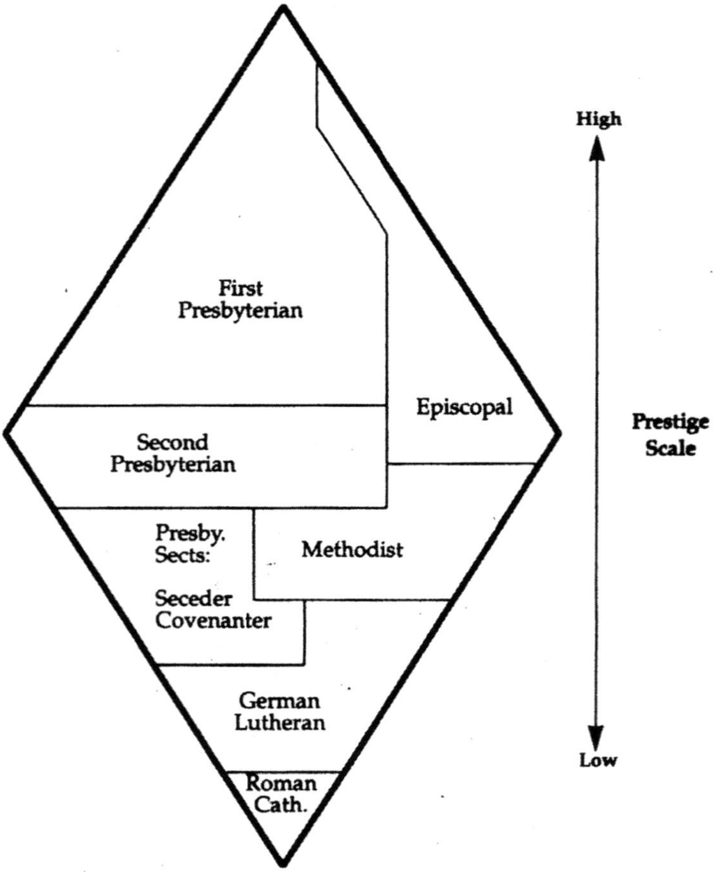

A prestige scale of Pittsburgh's religions. *Courtesy of Dr. Joseph Rishel.*

difficult to determine why Pittsburgh was different from other American cities in this respect; perhaps the answer was structural, in that Presbyterians topped the religious prestige scale, or perhaps it was the character of Bishop O'Connor or the conscience of "a Liberty St. Merchant" that was critical. In the final analysis, though, it was the forbearance of the people of Pittsburgh and the vigilance of the Irish that made a difference.

Speaking of vigilance, lest the reader think that religious intolerance is all in the past, we should consider an AOH newsletter from February 2000 that urged the Irish of Pittsburgh to write or call their congressmen to protest the treatment of Father Timothy O'Brien, who had been recommended for House chaplain. O'Brian would have been the first Catholic to ever serve in this distinguished and highly symbolic capacity, but members of the screening committee impugned his moral character because he was unmarried and questioned him about what he would wear on the House floor. House speaker Dennis Hastert, a man of impeccable moral character, selected instead the Presbyterian reverend Charles Parker Wright. The indignation of Pittsburgh's Irish Catholic constituency, along with that of concerned citizens across America, compelled Hastert to appoint instead the Reverend Daniel Coughlin, who became the first Catholic chaplain to the House of Representatives after two hundred years.

The Lost Shantytown of Iffly

Workers on the Pittsburgh and Steubenville Line often lived in places such as Iffly, a now forgotten Irish community once located on a minor tributary of Chartiers Creek known as Robinson Run. The "town" was born when the railroad work started in 1852, with the intent of reaching the Virginia state line. At that time, shacks sprang up on and near a farmstead owned by Gabriel Walker, who was descended from a founding family of the Noblestown Road area. The Walkers' tenant farmers were Samuel and Lilly Ann Kennedy, Presbyterians from Belfast. The Kennedys, in turn, acted as lord and lady of the manor to the shantytown Irish squatters, who squeezed in along the bottomland by Robinson Run. These "Paddy Irish" lived in about thirty dirt-floored and rough-boarded shacks along the tracks between the Rennerdale and Gregg stations. Historian Milton M. Allison has captured the spirit of Kennedy's overlordship of the nearly two hundred "tatterdemalion inhabitants" of his domain:

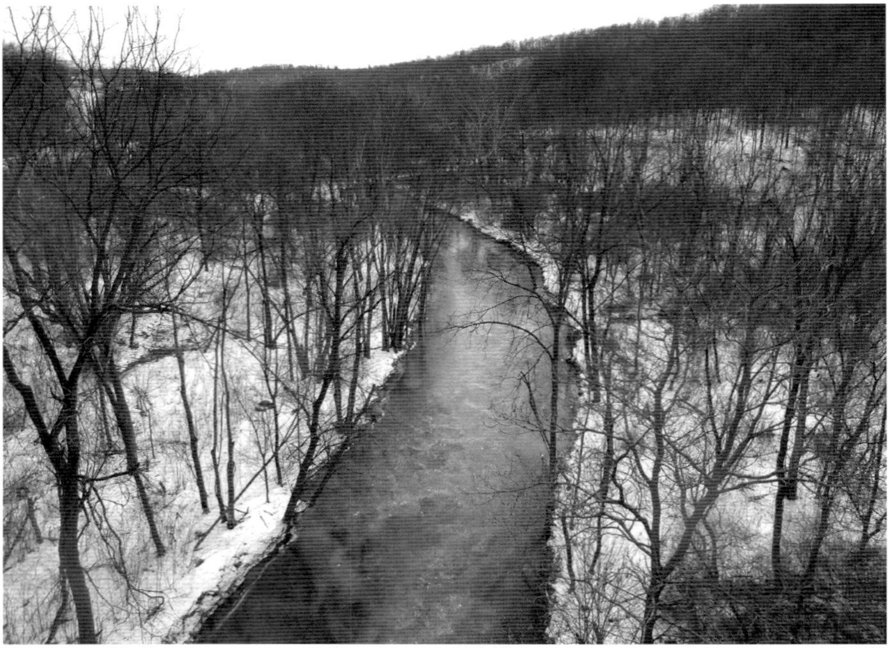

The site of the Iffly shantytown beneath the Nike Road Bridge in Collier Township. *Courtesy of Janis Ferrainolo.*

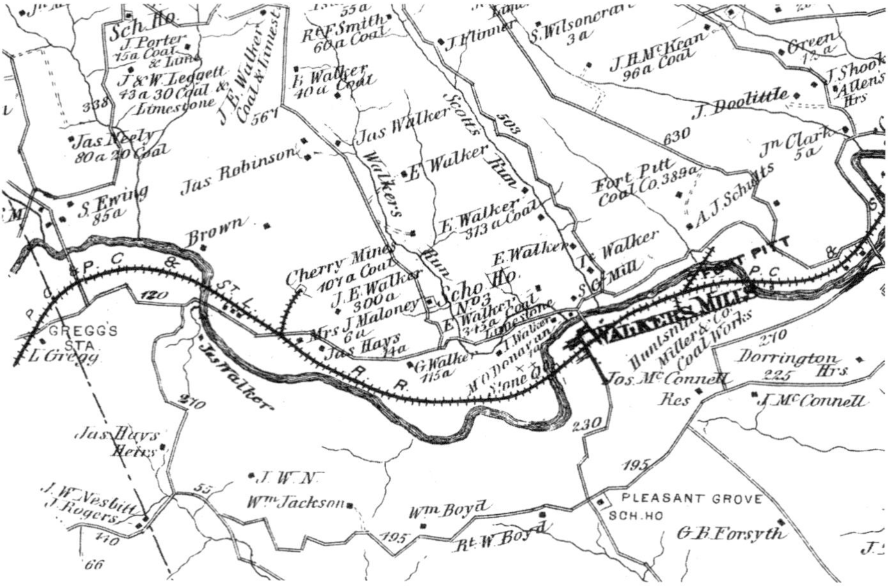

Collier Township in 1872, centered on Gabriel Walker's homestead. *From* G.M. Hopkins & Co., 1872 Atlas of Allegheny County, Pennsylvania.

> *His word was law in the camp and his warning, unheeded, brought swift judgment betimes. When Kennedy took notice that a new shanty had sprung up overnight in too close proximity to his potato patch, he would come civilly admonishing the new neighbor against pilfering his crop. "Shure an' we have our own praties comin' on" was the invariable retort, referring to an inadequate planting at the corner of the shanty. At the first undeniable offense came Kennedy, with his ladder and crowbar, and down came the roof and walls in short order. In impish glee the demolisher kept whistling the "Boyne Water" and other Orange airs while he carried his work to completion.*

Meanwhile, neighboring shantytown residents who had already learned their lessons raised no objections to the proceedings, for they knew from their own experience that the Kennedys gave food to the needy and nursed the sick. Their landlord may have been a Presbyterian heretic, but by all accounts, the shanty dwellers loved him. Samuel would even prepare coffins in his spare time, and Lilly would produce coffin liners and shrouds out of muslin. The death rate was high, as cholera, dysentery, smallpox, donnybrooks and murders took their toll. It also fell upon the Kennedys to cart home from Mansfield (now Carnegie) the "dead drunks," the inevitable

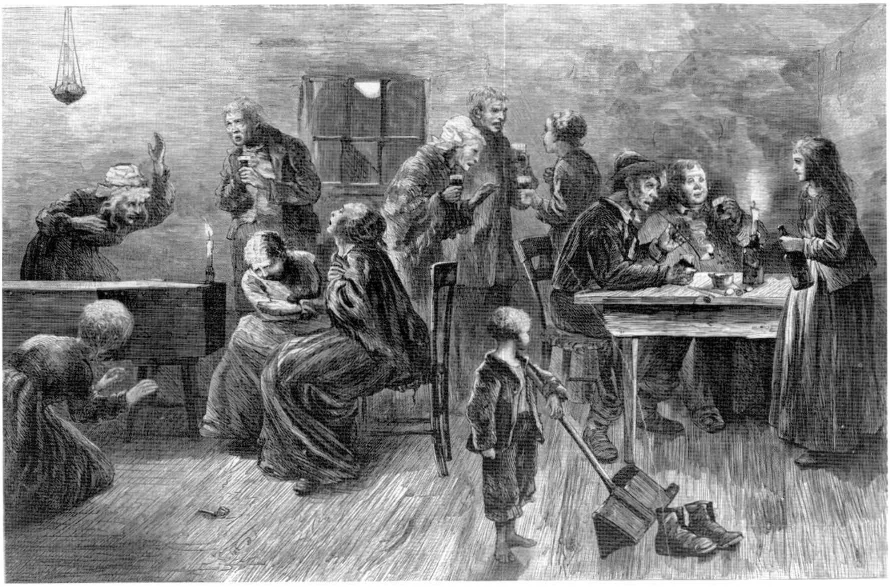

An Irish wake. *Courtesy of the Library of Congress.*

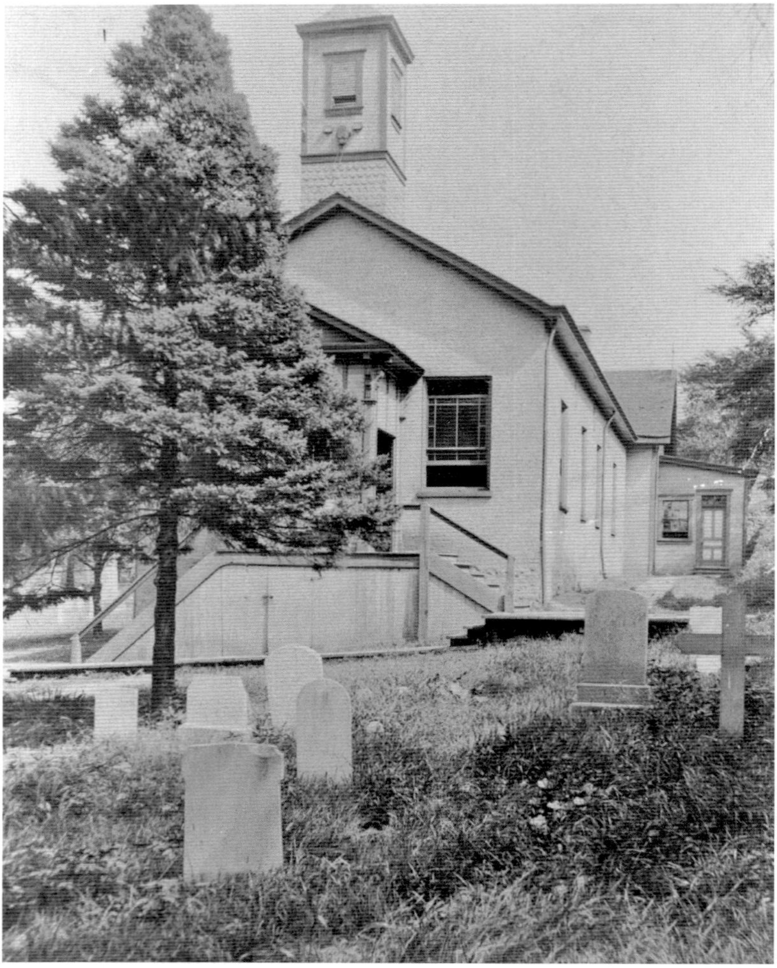

The original St. Phillip's Church around 1900. *Courtesy of the Catholic Historical Society.*

casualties of a wake, an eight-mile trip to St. Phillip's Church in Crafton and a mandatory refreshment pause in Carnegie on the return trip:

> *Alighting at the edge of the settlement, Kennedy began to assort and deliver his passengers. Shortly, each fellow in turn would be dragged out by the heels and dropped like a pitpost in the roadway before his shack. While the driver walked behind the wagon, the horses would repeatedly start and stop again until all the mourners were returned each to his own door.*

Apparently, having a "designated driver" is not a twentieth-century invention. Clergymen frequently denounced these excesses because they diverted money that should have paid for the Mass of the dead. The "paddy funeral" was not only costly but also disrespectful; male mourners commonly loitered outside the church and continued their drinking and ribald behavior rather than attend the services. However, this celebration was a deep-rooted tradition that served an important function in Irish folk culture; it was believed that merrymaking would appease the troublesome spirits of the "other world" at a moment when the boundary between the worlds was precariously thin. The Celtic tradition, like many others, saw danger in boundaries. Precautions had to be taken, and apparently drinking "spirits" or "the water of life" was a proven method for limiting otherworldly mischief, despite its evident worldly consequences.

Residents of Rennerdale also recalled that the "Paddy Irish" children were constantly fearful of sudden raids by other railroad construction camps. Many nights, dreading an assault, the entire population of Iffly would sleep in the woods on the hillsides behind the Kennedys' house. In the morning, men, women and children could be seen returning from their

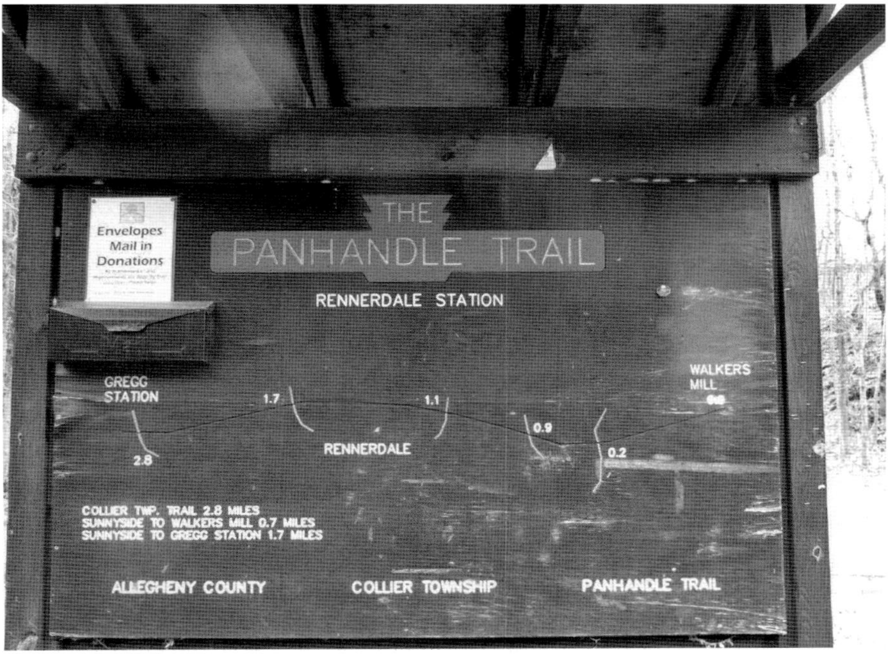

Panhandle Trail map at the site of Rennerdale Station. *Courtesy of Janis Ferrainolo.*

hiding places, carrying their dirty tics and bedclothes. Education for these children was the only way up and out, and fortunately they were accepted at the local Walker School, which was strongly Presbyterian but permitted its Catholic students to read what little Catholic religious material they could afford. Many of the residents went on to become property owners in Carnegie or nearby towns; others might have moved west with the railroads. The Irish Catholics were referred to as the "fish-eating Paddy Irish," but this probably referred to poverty-driven necessity as much as penitential dietary practice. In any event, both the fish and the Irish were displaced by pollution and industrial development within a few years of the railroad building, and nothing remains of the shanties of Iffly. Today, even the railroad is gone, and if you see people running along the creek, they're not being chased by shillelagh-wielding Fardowns—they're just taking a jog along the Panhandle Trail.

Part III

IRISH PITTSBURGH IN THE CIVIL WAR, 1861–1865

American concerns over Irish immigration soon took a back seat to the tremendous issue of slavery that threatened to rip apart the Union. A total of 426,286 Pennsylvanians served in the Union forces in 270 regiments and several detached companies of the Volunteer Army, along with the navy. For Irish Americans, the turning point of their early years in the United States would be the American Civil War. Over 140,000 enlisted in the Union army, while others in the South enrolled in the Confederate ranks. Most men enlisted in locally based regiments, but five Irish regiments fought for the Union; together they constituted the famous Irish Brigade, and they suffered staggering casualties over the course of the war. In all, 4,000 men of the Irish Brigade were killed or wounded, a number that exceeded the total enlistment of the brigade at any time; valor and gallantry in the face of industrial killing capacity had a steep price. Extensive recruiting was needed to maintain brigade strength, and it can be said safely that by the end of the war, despite continuous unbroken service, the brigade was not as it was at the beginning. In fact, toward the end of the war, the Irish Brigade was 18 percent Pennsylvania Dutch—there was no other way to replace men who were killed, wounded or missing in action. Pennsylvania's 116th Regiment was added to the Irish Brigade in the fall of 1862, and consequently, there is no evidence that the 116th had its own regimental flag or colors. Initially under the command of General Francis Thomas Meagher, the Irish earned a reputation for dependability and bravery in battles such as Bull Run, Antietam and Gettysburg. At Fredericksburg, for instance, casualties

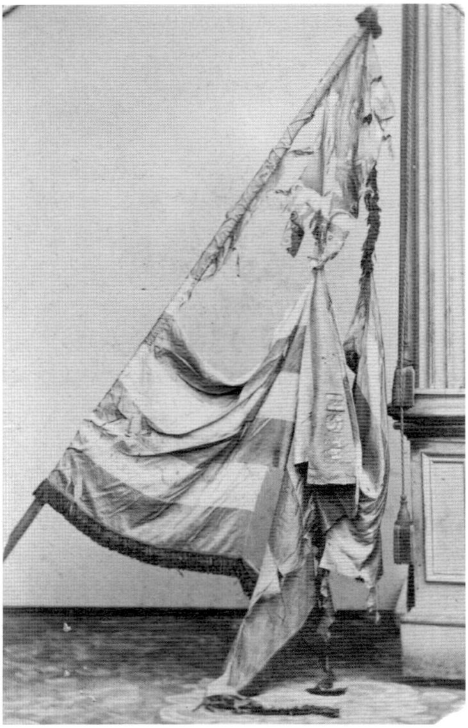

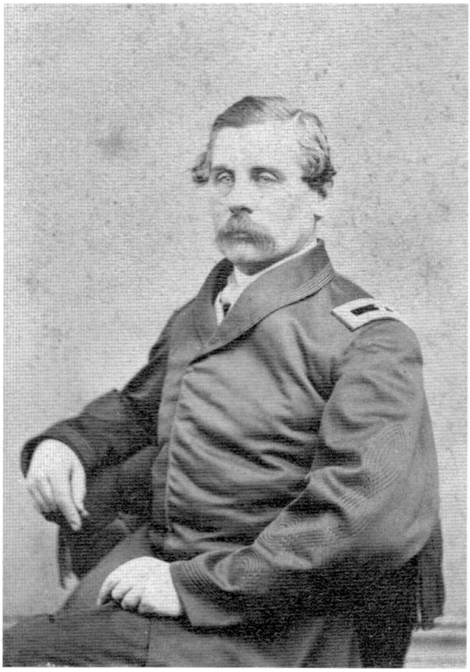

in the assault on the stone wall at Marye's Heights exceeded 40 percent. Often the Irish felt that their service to the country was underappreciated, however, and Meagher was eventually fired in a controversial dispute.

In the spring of 1864, Pittsburgh provided new recruits to replenish the 116th, and Companies H, I and K were recruited from Pittsburgh and surrounding areas, particularly Fayette County. This effort brought the regiment up to full strength for the first time. The new recruits may have entered service late in the war, but they enlisted just in time for the brutal spring campaign of 1864, in which Grant's overall strategy was to slowly grind down Confederate forces in a war of attrition that was unwinnable for the South. The new recruits performed well in the Battle of the Wilderness and at Spotsylvania, and many Irish Pittsburghers lost their lives in picket duty at Petersburg. However, Grant's war of attrition took a heavy toll on the Irish Brigade, and in July 1864, the brigade was broken up. The 116th

Top: The flag of the Pennsylvania 116th Volunteers. *Courtesy of Michael Kraus.*

Left: Thomas Francis Meagher. *Courtesy of Michael Kraus.*

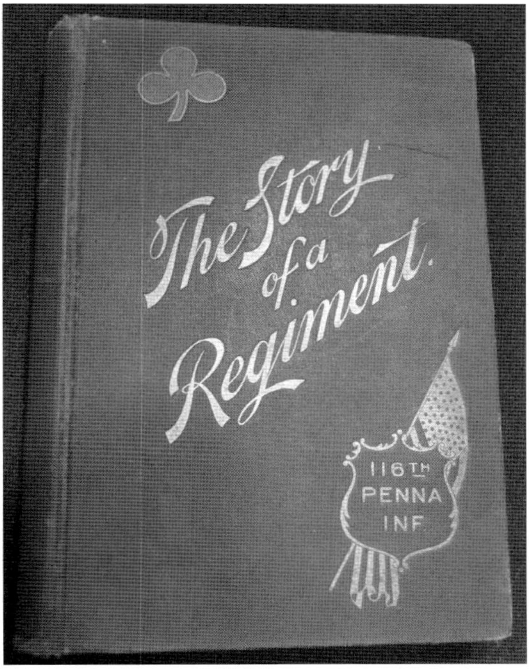

Right: St. Clair Augustine Mullholland's regimental history of the 116th Pennsylvania Volunteers. *Courtesy of Michael Kraus.*

Below: Mulholland's signature in his history of the 116th, owned by veteran Samuel A. Clear of Washington County. *Courtesy of Michael Kraus.*

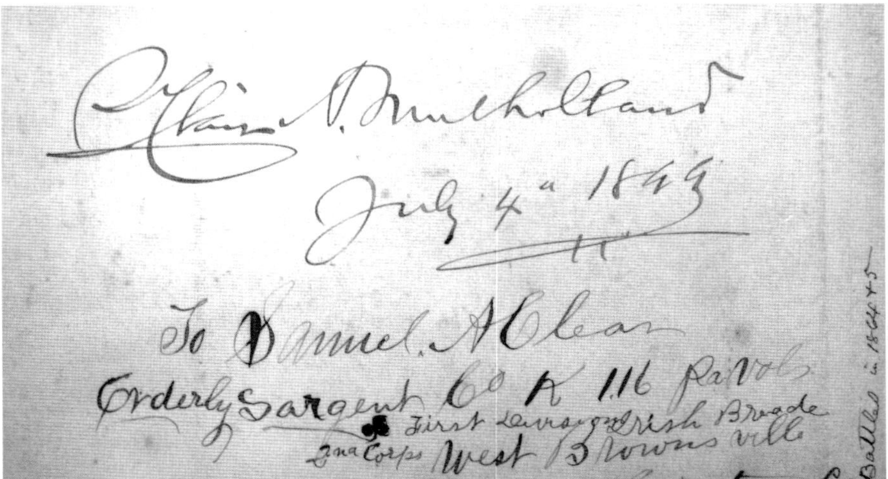

Pennsylvania transferred to the 4th Brigade of the 1st Division, 2nd Army Corps, where it remained until the end of the war.

Most of western Pennsylvania's recruits who replenished the Irish Brigade hailed from Fayette County, and a few examples will suffice. The Chisholm brothers of Uniontown, Daniel and Alexander, both served in Company K of the 116th Regiment, although their cousins, the Chisholms of Maryland, were divided and fought in both the Union and Confederate armies. Daniel Chisholm, the eldest son of Alexander and Mary Ann Chisholm, was born near Uniontown in 1845. He worked as a clerk in a Uniontown dry goods store from 1861 until February 1864, when he enlisted in Company K and saw sixteen months of dangerous service. At the Battle of the Wilderness, his cap was shot from his head, and he saw action at Spotsylvania Courthouse, Cold Harbor, Poe River and several other battles. At Petersburg, he was wounded in the leg, and at Strawberry Plains, he received a slight wound but avoided capture. He was honorably discharged on June 9, 1865. After the war, he continued working as a drug clerk in Uniontown for fifteen years until opening his own dry goods business, owning a series of progressively larger stores. He was an active Presbyterian and Republican in the Uniontown community for many years. Alexander Chisholm was born near Uniontown in 1846 and first enlisted in the 48th Regiment when the Morgan Raiders invaded Ohio in the summer of 1863. In February 1864, he enlisted for three years in Company K of the 116th Regiment and was engaged in twenty-two battles and skirmishes without any serious injury. He was honorably discharged in July 1865 and set up shop in Uniontown as a carpenter, subsequently becoming one of the leading contractors and

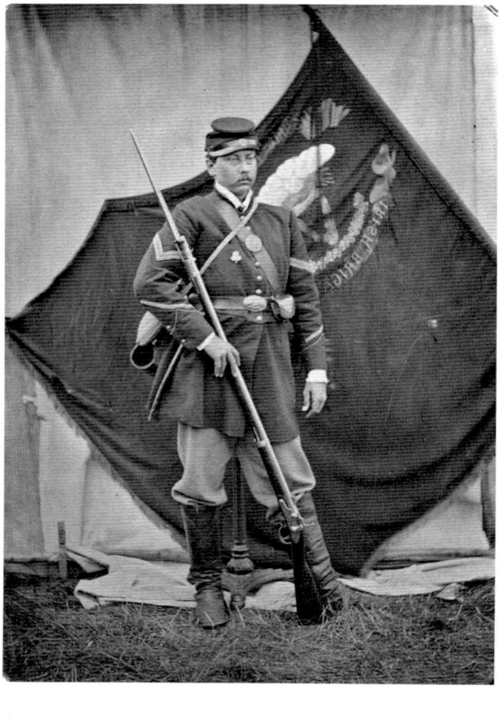

A reenactor of the Pennsylvania 116th Volunteers. *Courtesy of Michael Kraus.*

builders of Uniontown and Fayette County. After traveling in the far West for a year, Alexander returned to Uniontown, where he became one of the first uniformed police officers, tasked with preventing street fights and rioting. Politically, he moved from Republican to Socialist as he grew older. Thomas Thorndell, a shoemaker from Uniontown who enlisted in Company K, was not so fortunate; he served for three years and was killed in the last major battle at Five Forks on March 31, 1865.

Although no battles took place in Pittsburgh, the governor of Pennsylvania was Andrew Gregg Curtin, a lawyer of Irish Presbyterian descent who defeated Henry D. Foster of Westmoreland County in 1861. Curtin had joined the new Republican Party in 1860 and was one of Lincoln's staunchest supporters. He established the first and largest Civil War camp and was the first governor to send troops, known as "The First Defenders," to protect Washington, D.C., which was perilously close to the Rebel state of Virginia. The 155th Regiment was raised from western Pennsylvania early in the war, and we shall look at one soldier, Charles McKenna, as an example of life in that regiment.

Charles McKenna of the 155th Regiment

The McKenna family were Irish Catholic residents of what is now downtown Pittsburgh. In 1832, Charles's grandfather Hugh McKenna gave up tenant farming on the estate of the Earl of Caledon in Ireland. Hugh McKenna immigrated to Pittsburgh from County Tyrone with six sons and four daughters. One of Hugh's sons, James McKenna, died in 1846 and was survived by six children, including Charles. Charles McKenna was born in Pennsylvania on October 1, 1844, a year before his father's death. Normally, the death of the main breadwinner in the family would have meant dire poverty. A common alternative for widows was to run a cigar or grog shop that was a front for other vices. Anna McKenna was fortunate in that she owned a property at 911 Penn Street and ran it as a boardinghouse, a common and not disrespectable practice. The 1860 census indicates that the widowed Anna McKenna, age fifty, owned a residence with twenty-one occupants, including eight people with the last name McKenna. According to adjacent census pages, the "Old Galway" neighborhood was almost entirely Irish in 1860, with a few German residents. All residents of the boardinghouse had Irish surnames, with the exception of a Stewart. On the date of June

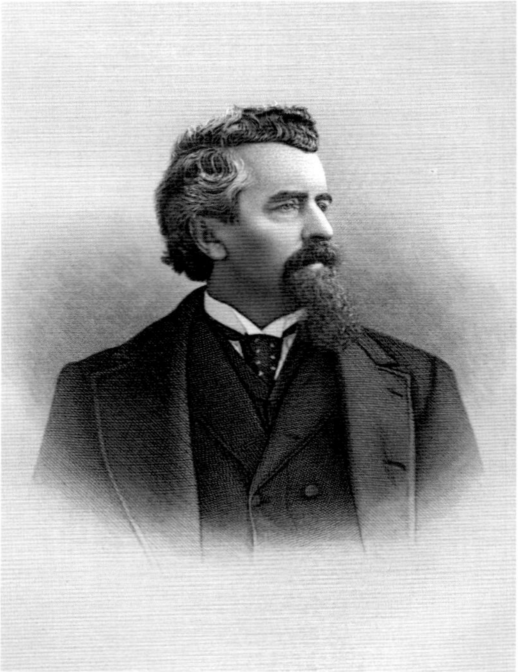

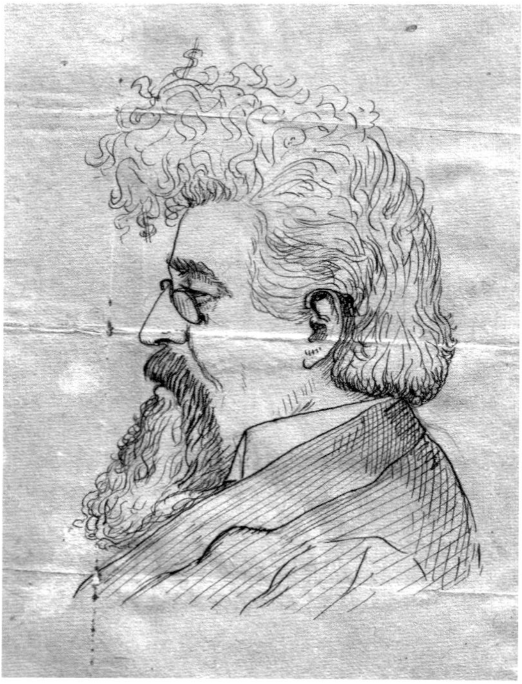

14, 1860, Charles McKenna was listed in the census as a lithographer, age sixteen. At age fourteen, Charles had been apprenticed to the leading Pittsburgh lithographer, William Schuchman, but war broke out before his instruction was finished.

In 1862, in response to President Lincoln's call for 300,000 men, sixteen-year-old Charles F. McKenna enlisted in the 155th Regiment of Pennsylvania Volunteers. He was mustered into military service on August 22, 1862, and mustered out on June 2, 1865. The 155th was one of the few regiments chosen to receive Lee's surrender at Appomattox, and McKenna served with this distinguished regiment for the duration of the war. A competent and literate soldier, McKenna was eventually selected to serve as a clerk in the fifth army headquarters. During his three years of service,

Top: A lithograph of Charles McKenna. *Author's collection.*

Left: Charles McKenna's self-portrait. *Courtesy of Soldiers and Sailors Memorial Hall Archives.*

McKenna never missed a day of duty and never received a furlough. His letters indicate that he was patient and diligent, neither seeking nor refusing promotion, and his attitude of unassuming competence presumably led to his detail as clerk. Charles survived the war, eventually became a Pittsburgh judge and served briefly as a federal judge in Puerto Rico shortly after its annexation from Spain. His younger brother Bernard would become mayor of Pittsburgh from 1893 to 1896. Charles F. McKenna's experience is a good example of an Irish Catholic's journey from outsider to pillar of society in nineteenth-century America. Later in life, McKenna was instrumental in the construction of the Soldiers and Sailors Memorial Hall in Pittsburgh and served on its board of directors.

The men of the 155th Regiment saw extensive action in the course of the war, partaking in thirty-two battles. In 1863 alone, they crossed and recrossed the Rappahannock fourteen times. During the entire war, they were either engaged with Robert E. Lee's troops or guarding against Confederate raids across the Potomac. In the winter of 1863–64, they were stationed at Warrenton Junction, Virginia, to protect the integrity of the Orange & Alexandria Railroad. They narrowly averted certain slaughter in a proposed engagement at Mine Run in late 1863 when General Warren declined to assault well-positioned Confederate troops, fearing a repeat of Fredericksburg. General Meade concurred with Warren's assessment, and both sides settled into winter quarters.

McKenna's handwriting and vocabulary were remarkable, and both showed improvements in his later letters. While in winter quarters, McKenna resumed his studies under Sergeant George P. Fulton, who later served as principal of the Highland Public Schools in Pittsburgh. Truly noticeable are the elaborate signatures McKenna devises in his letters as the war progresses. His skill at addressing letters with ornamental flourish was eventually in great demand. In fact, McKenna jokingly remarked that calligraphy was his great contribution to the war effort: "For my skill I often when visiting get the gratuitous task of directing a half dozen envelopes, with the request to put some 'extras' on. It was for this work I suppose I am indebted to Sackett for the Maltese cross."

Soldiers always needed money, and McKenna used his drawing skills to that end. While in their winter quarters from February to April 1863, he produced a sketch of Camp Humphries, near Falmouth, Virginia. It was then lithographed by William Schuchman, his former employer in Pittsburgh, and McKenna sold these lithographs in camp. The sketches were popular because Camp Humphries was the first real quarters for the 155th Regiment and a great improvement over the unsanitary conditions they had

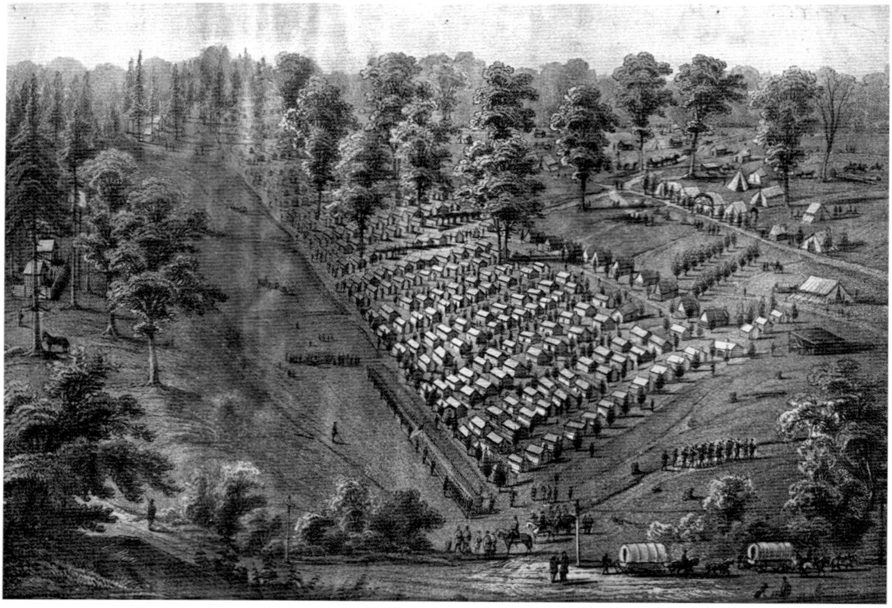

McKenna's lithographed sketch of Camp Humphries. *Courtesy of Soldiers and Sailors Memorial Hall Archives.*

experienced during the previous fall and winter. However, McKenna's little enterprise was a mixed success; upon hearing false reports that they would be moving out soon, he sold off the lithographs quickly at a reduced price of twenty-five cents. Instead, they stayed in camp during the early spring of 1863. Demand for his sketch of Camp Humphries remained high, so another order for lithographs was placed. The 155th left camp on April 27, 1863, to begin marching to Chancellorsville, where it helped avert a rout of Union forces by Stonewall Jackson. It suffered few casualties at Chancellorsville because it was made up of reserves, not assault troops.

There were many problems faced by an aspiring artist in a military camp. The first problem was artistic; to properly sketch the camp at Warrenton Station, Virginia, would have required viewing it from an elevation, but no such natural promontory existed near the camp. Repeated attempts to sketch from an imaginary bird's-eye view were deemed unsatisfactory. Moreover, McKenna described the problems of dwelling in a busy, often chaotic army camp:

> *Another great obstacle to my finishing or executing a drawing satisfactorily is our furniture is very unstable and besides, our house is a great resort for*

> *visitors who probably will get boisterous at the moment I am on delicate points, shove against me, probably upset myself drawing ink chair and table. If not this a crowd assembles and a "Euchre deck" is brought forth and noise and confusion prevails.*

In a later letter from the night of September 22, 1864, McKenna seemed pleased to "have the whole Asst. Adjt. Genl's office to myself."

McKenna rarely complained openly about the life of a soldier. However, his evaluations of officer competence were straightforward and clear assessments of their abilities and weaknesses. He always considered whether officers were liked by the men they led, although aloofness in itself was not a fault in his eyes. Fairness, sobriety and understanding of drills were among the essential traits McKenna valued in his officers. It must be noted that some of McKenna's friends from home were hardly paragons of sobriety; Sergeant Hughey McGimpsey, for example, was known as "Fish." Officers who looked after the well-being of their men, even at the risk of court-martial, were especially respected. A tantalizingly small letter fragment referred to the travails of Colonel Allen, who refused to remove his sick men from their quarters in private houses that had been appropriated from people of dubious loyalty.

In his letters home, McKenna repeatedly described the need to learn the new bayonet and skirmish drills without providing a clear explanation. The old drills from the Napoleonic era involved the disciplined formation of a "hollow square." A resolute group of kneeling men, with fixed bayonets pointed outward, would impale cavalry instead of being run down by them. However, the Confederate cavalry of Fitz Hugh Lee and "Jeb" Stuart declined to attack such massed infantry, so new tactics were called for. A new drill known as the "Zouave" was introduced, and special loose-fitting uniforms were modeled after those of French fighters in Algeria, a reward to the men for attaining proficiency at drills. The Zouave outfit was so distinctive that it was impossible to escape the attention of provost guards if a soldier were to fall out of ranks or engage in any forbidden activity. The week the Zouave uniforms were issued, McKenna sketched a soldier wearing one in camp, one of his few original sketches to have survived.

In his letters, McKenna evaluated the morale and quality of his fellow soldiers; many of the early volunteers were unfit for service, became ill and were sent home by the end of 1862. This was literally an on-the-ground assessment; they had no tents or gum rubber blankets in October 1862 in Maryland. Later in the war, new recruits were enticed by an enlistment

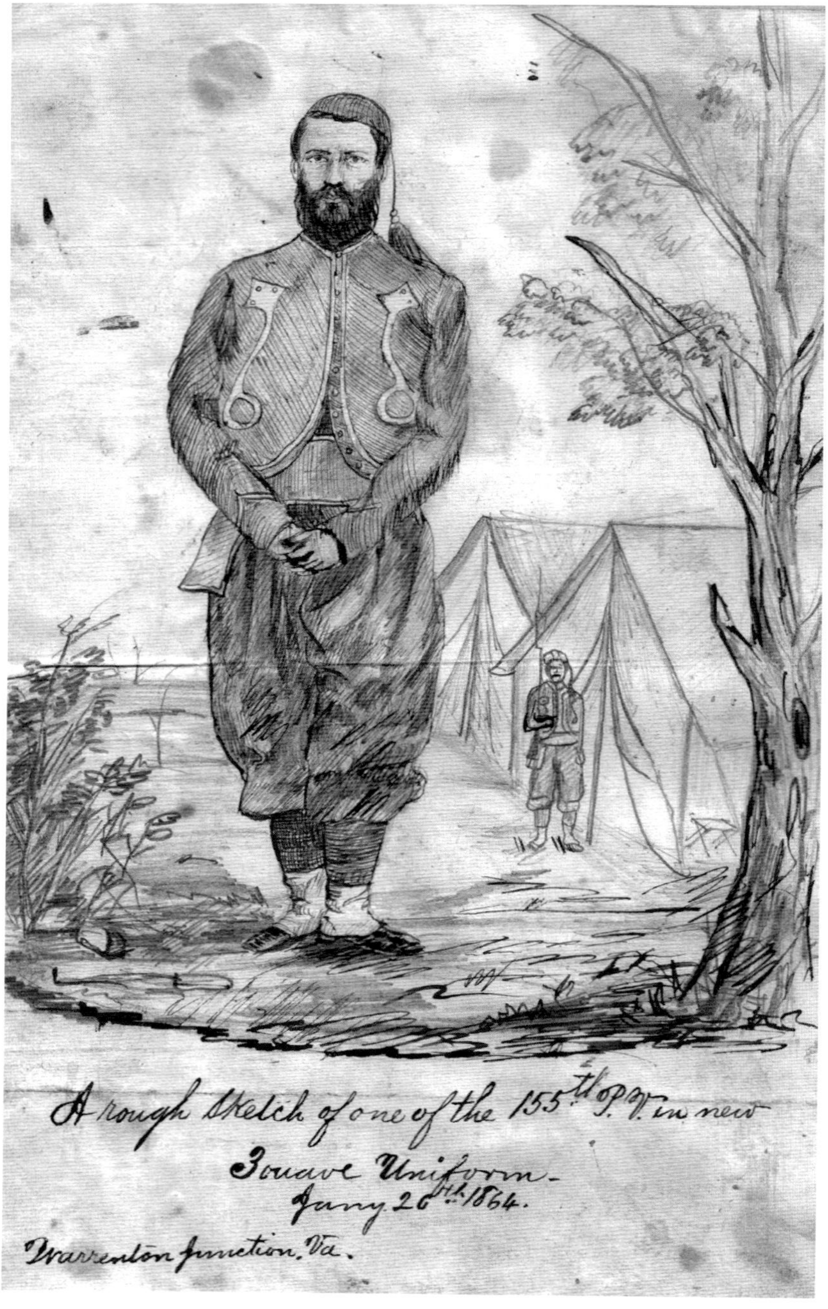

McKenna's sketch of the new Zouave uniform. *Courtesy of Soldiers and Sailors Memorial Hall Archives.*

bounty, and McKenna was not pleased with the caliber of men this attracted—school boys and old men, again, likely to succumb to disease. Even worse, there were many bounty jumpers among the new enlistees who would collect the enlistment bounty but desert at the first opportunity, often across Confederate lines. Consequently, raw recruits were forbidden picket and guard duty. According to McKenna:

> *Two of our regt. bounty jumpers deserted from picket the other night to the enemy, and to deprive others of this opportunity, no recruits are allowed to go on picket, and the Colonel will not allow them to be placed on guard because they have not the Zouave uniform. This throws the duty on all the old members who are few in number, and occasions no little complaint.*

Draftees and early volunteers such as McKenna were not pleased with the policy of paying men to enlist. Furthermore, rich men were allowed to pay $300, a small fortune for recent immigrants, to hire a substitute to fight in their place. McKenna clearly expressed his opinion that the bounty was wrong-headed; the Union needed men, not money, and the treasury could print in one day the "greenbacks" collected in a year from men of means who could afford to pay $300.

In an 1864 letter, McKenna hoped that Pittsburgh would not be attacked in the forthcoming campaign. Instead he wished a Rebel scourge upon the German farmers of eastern Pennsylvania who had ill treated the Union army the previous year. He wrote, "They have done very little for the country so far and should be made to suffer." As the 155th Regiment entered Pennsylvania in pursuit of Robert E. Lee's army, prosperous farmers offered milk, bread, pies, etc. for sale. Many of the young farmers appeared perfectly fit for military service, and the Union troops resented the mercenary activities of the farmers they were rushing to defend. Later, local farmers repeatedly demanded payment for straw taken as bedding for Union field hospitals both during and after the three-day Battle of Gettysburg. In the face of such callous indifference to suffering, Major Pearson threatened to court-martial the farmers for treason and send the 155th Regiment to destroy their barns.

A good example of the dedication of Irish soldiers from Pittsburgh is the fact that several members of the 155th Regiment defended Little Round Top while barefoot. After a lengthy forced march from Culpepper, their feet were too blistered and swollen to wear their boots. Although given passes and instructions to go to the rear, McKenna and several others insisted on following their comrades into position. McKenna and his Pittsburgh friend Jim O'Neill were on Pennsylvania soil and were determined to fight despite their condition. Union troops on Little Round Top were subject to sniper fire from Confederate sharpshooters located in Devil's Den, but the 155th Regiment was unable to reciprocate. Its men were armed with old muskets from the Harpers Ferry Arsenal that had an effective range of only twenty yards. They obeyed orders to withhold fire until the Rebels were close enough for their muskets to be effective. The lack of fire from the 155th Regiment caused the Confederates to mistake its position for a gap in the Union line. When the Confederates attempted to take advantage of this perceived weakness, however, they were instead repelled by a massive point-blank volley. The authors of *The Maltese Cross* conservatively estimated that two thousand Union troops were unfit to pursue Lee's army after Gettysburg because of the damage inflicted on their feet while rapidly marching to confront Lee.

The letters of Charles McKenna reveal the thoughts of a bright young man who was fortunate to survive the war without injury. His correspondence presented a soldier's-eye view of the war and of the conditions and morale within the ranks of the 155th Regiment. While better known as an artist at the time, his interest in things political foreboded his future legal career. In May 1865, he began studying law in the offices of Mitchell & Palmer, and on October 17, 1868, Charles McKenna was admitted to the bar. In 1872, he married Virginia White, sister of a prominent Pittsburgh judge. The McKennas had no children, and Charles eventually formed a law partnership with his nephews E.J and J. Frank McKenna. He became actively involved in national politics and served as a delegate to the Democratic National Convention in 1880. General Hancock, a Civil War commander, was nominated at the convention, and his campaign was supported by McKenna. After serving as a federal judge in Puerto Rico from 1904 to 1906, he resumed his service as a judge in Pittsburgh. He was still a sitting judge when he died of a heart attack at age seventy-eight on December 22, 1922. Whenever he was asked why his artwork was never publicly exhibited, McKenna would reply: "I'm in the law and to appear as an artist might seem confusing."

Theresa and Edward O'Brien

Colonel Edward O'Brien of New Castle, Pennsylvania, is another example of an Irish Pittsburgher who served several enlistments with distinction in the Pennsylvania Volunteers. Edward was born in Pittsburgh on October 10, 1823, and was the eldest son of Thomas O'Brien, who had come to America around 1800 and moved to Pittsburgh by 1822. At age fifteen, Edward became a molder's apprentice at the firm of Bollman and Garrison, and this became his trade. After the death of Thomas O'Brien, the family relocated to New Castle. When the Mexican War broke out, O'Brien enlisted in the "Irish Greens" in June 1846. The Irish Greens, a Pittsburgh company about which little is known, saw action at Veracruz, Cerro Gordo, Chapultepec, Garita de Belen and the pass of La Hoya.

O'Brien was married to Theresa O'Donnell on April 20 1861, and the following day, he started service in the field as captain of Company F of the 12th Pennsylvania Volunteers. This company was mustered out in August 1861; initial enlistment terms were short because in the early enthusiasm for war, few people expected a long and bitter conflict. Responding to an appeal for troops from Governor Curtin, O'Brien recruited Company D of the 134th Pennsylvania Volunteers for nine months' service. Back then, one way to become an officer was to recruit a company, and this subcontracting of recruitment by the army gave many fighting units a strong and highly local connection.

During this enlistment, his wife, Theresa (O'Donnell) O'Brien, went to war with him. This was not as uncommon as it sounds today; many wives followed the army to wash clothes and perform other camp chores but then headed for safety when battle was imminent. Women were both a burden and a blessing for troops in the field. They required extra protection, but their service freed up men for other tasks and fighting. O'Brien's training as a molder and later foundry work suggest that he was working class and not wealthy, but his previous experience qualified him as an officer. Theresa O'Brien was therefore not expected to perform chores because her husband was an officer and not an enlisted man. They lived together in the shared tent they called "home," and it is doubtful that they would have enjoyed the luxuries that wealthy officers brought to the field, such as maids, servants, elaborate furnishings and even personal kitchens. Theresa chose a risky undertaking, as disease was a major killer in the field, especially before the acceptance of germ theory, the invention of antibiotics and the development of sanitary procedures. Furthermore, Confederate raids were a real possibility. Her diary

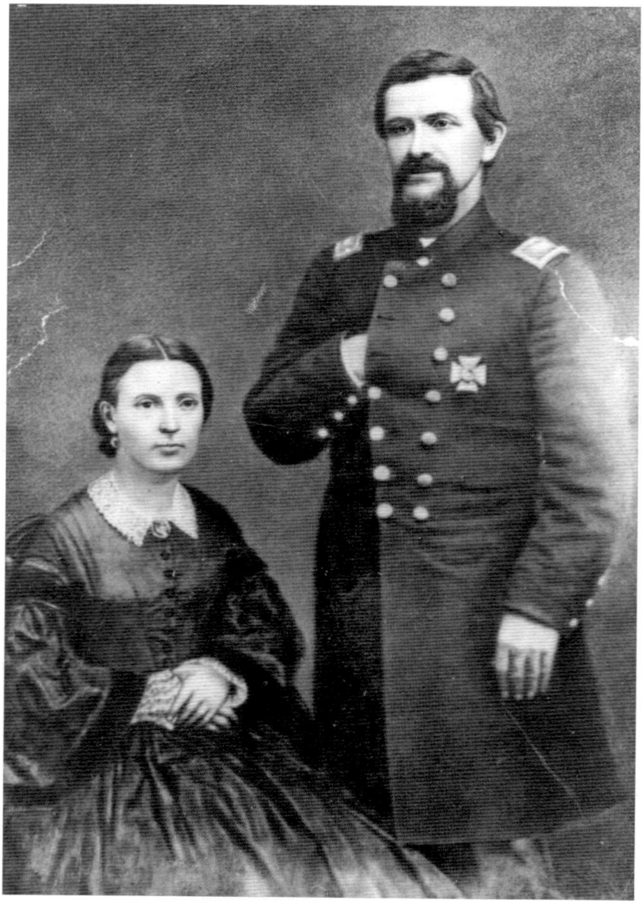

Theresa and Edward O'Brien. *Courtesy of Detre Library and Archives at John Heinz History Center.*

occasionally places her on the fringes of battle action, and she witnessed plenty of grisly aftermath from several battles. One thing that stands out is her anguish at being separated from her husband at a safe location, such as a nearby hotel, while waiting for news from a battle.

The chances that Edward would not return were shockingly high. At Fredericksburg, fifteen futile assaults were launched on Marye's Heights and the "terrible stone wall." The landscape provided virtually no protection from General Longstreet's artillery fire. Each successive charge melted away in the withering fire, and not a single Union soldier reached the stone wall. Of the 12,600 Federal soldiers killed, wounded or missing at Fredericksburg,

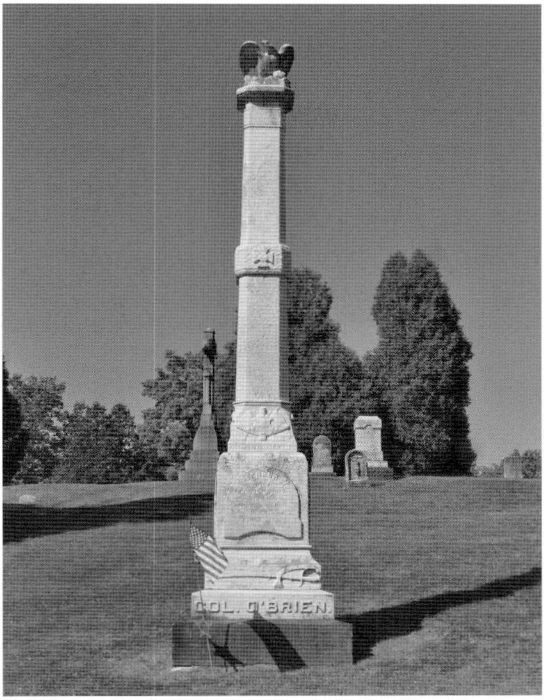

Right: O'Brien Monument, St. Mary's Cemetery, New Castle. *Courtesy of Janis Ferrainolo.*

Below: O'Brien Monument, St. Mary's Cemetery, New Castle. *Courtesy of Janis Ferrainolo.*

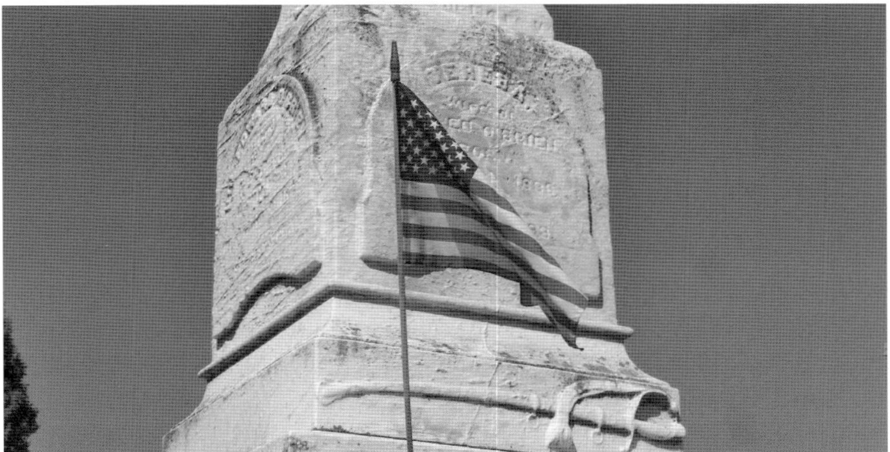

nearly two-thirds fell in front of the stone wall atop Marye's Heights. After the Battle of Fredericksburg, General Humphreys, the division commander, praised O'Brien: "Under my own eye he rode in front of his regiment, and literally led it in the last charge on the stone wall, at Fredericksburg, just before dark on December 13th. He is in every way reliable, a good soldier and gallant leader, always attentive to duty, careful and considerate of those under his command, prompt in execution."

During this battle, O'Brien had one of many close scrapes. While he was standing up in the stirrups to get a better view of the action, a Minié ball zipped between his legs, tearing his pants and removing part of his saddle. His younger brother Thomas O'Brien of Company D was not so fortunate and was killed in this battle. At the Battle of Chancellorsville, Edward O'Brien was similarly commended by General Tyler and was just as fortunate; despite his heavy exposure to enemy fire, he was unhurt, but his hat and clothes were riddled by bullets.

The 134th Regiment was mustered out of service on May 26, 1865, but O'Brien did not enjoy the postwar peace for long. On February 3, 1866, he lost his left eye in an explosion at the R.W Cunningham foundry. Unable to work, he suffered from severe depression and was admitted to Dixmont Hospital, where he died in October 1877. Theresa rejoined him in 1883. The O'Briens were long-standing members of St. Mary's congregation in New Castle, and an impressive yet weathered monument marks the burial place of Theresa and Edward O'Brien in that church's cemetery.

The Allegheny Arsenal Disaster

Pennsylvania played a key role during the Civil War. Its industrial enterprise and natural resources were essential factors in the economic strength of the Northern cause. The railroad system, iron and steel industry and agricultural wealth were vital to the war effort. One key component of this industrial infrastructure was the Allegheny Arsenal, established during the War of 1812 and situated on thirty-eight acres of land in Lawrenceville, at Butler Avenue and Fortieth Street. The election of 1860 and the subsequent uproar by the Southern states brought unexpected changes across the country. Tensions were high everywhere, and Pittsburgh was no exception. The Allegheny Arsenal was a large and important part of Pittsburgh's economy and was still one of the best arsenals in the country.

Commanded by John Symington, the arsenal continued to supply the army throughout the country, including the South, through 1860. As the country moved toward war, Pittsburghers became angry when Symington continued to supply army stations in the South, despite the fact that he was merely following orders. Many viewed this as supplying the enemy, and this fueled a growing anti-secessionist sentiment. Symington remained a controversial figure, dogged by questions about his loyalty. It was no help that his son joined the Confederate army and his daughter dared to wear a Confederate rosette in church. During the war, the arsenal served as a supply and manufacturing center of cartridges for the troops in the West, and much of the work under Symington's command was performed by women of Irish ancestry. They would pay dearly.

The placid location of the arsenal's site today belies the horror of September 17, 1862, when 156 women were busy in a single-story building known as the Laboratory rolling, pinching, tying and bundling rifle cartridges filled with bullets and black powder. Women as young as age fourteen performed these repetitive tasks with stiff backs and bleary eyes for $0.50 to $1.10 a day. This was considered good pay for women and was more than what an army private was paid; there was a strong incentive, aside from patriotism, to perform such dangerous work. There was a great demand for ammunition in anticipation of the Battle of Antietam, and the women worked at a feverish pace. Why were women performing such dangerous work? Able-bodied men were needed for other tasks or at the front, and boys had a rather distressing tendency to play with matches.

It was payday, and around two o'clock in the afternoon, many of the young women were collecting their pay or in the yard. Despite precautions, it appears that an iron wagon wheel struck a spark on a paving stone that ignited spilled powder. There followed a "sheet of flame" and three enormous explosions that destroyed the Laboratory. Many workers were incinerated where they stood as the fire spread to other rooms and buildings.

One of the survivors was the operations superintendent, Alexander McBride, an Irish Catholic immigrant. He escaped out a window but failed to rescue his fourteen-year-old daughter, Kate McBride, as a flaming ceiling collapsed on her work area. The *Pittsburgh Evening Chronicle* recounts the "agonizing screams of relatives and friends discovering the remains of some loved ones whose humble earnings contributed to their comfort." According to the account, "There was not a piece of clothing left on a majority of the victims, and mangled and disjointed as they were it was impossible to identify them. The very stockings were torn from their feet, rings from their

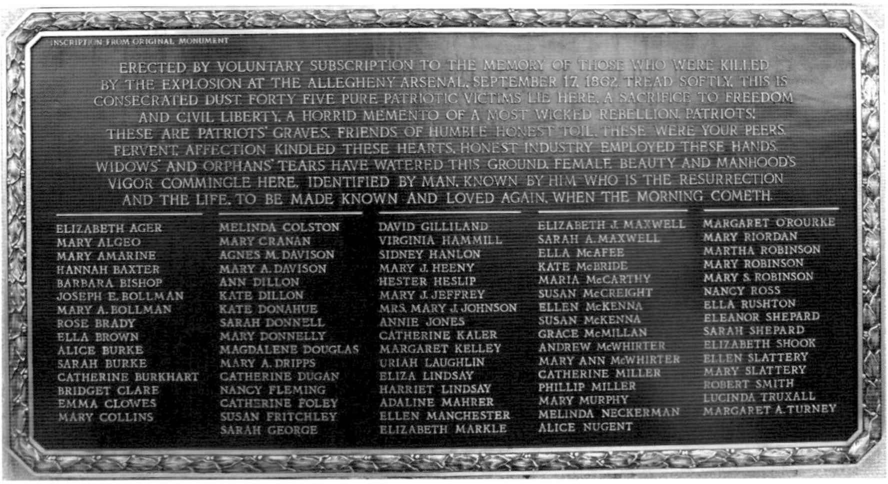

Arsenal Explosion Memorial, Allegheny Cemetery, Lawrenceville. *Courtesy of Janis Ferrainolo.*

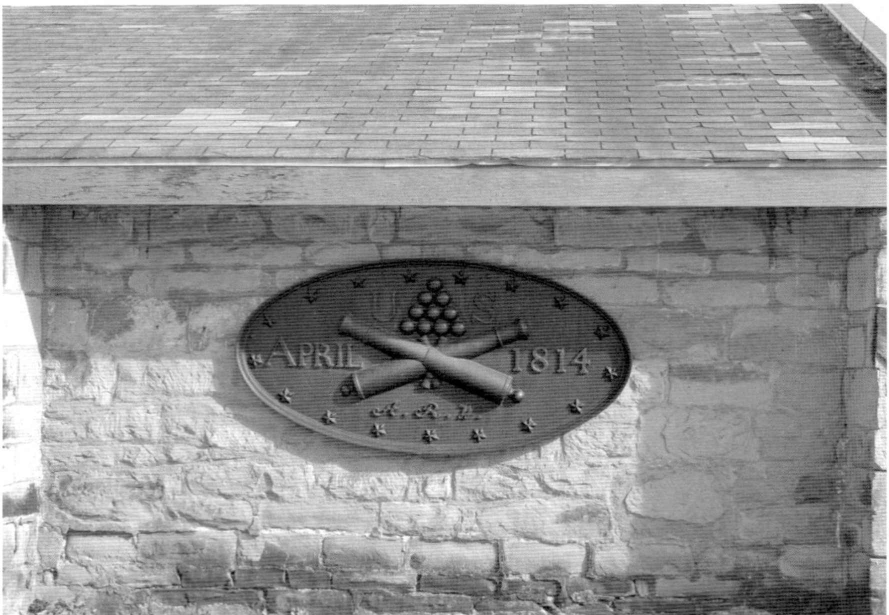

The original powder magazine from the Allegheny Arsenal. *Courtesy of Janis Ferrainolo.*

fingers, and in some instances nothing but a headless trunk remained." A few victims were recognized by their hair or scraps of their dresses, but forty-five people could not be identified. Some simply vanished. Unidentified victims were buried in a common grave in Allegheny Cemetery. A total of seventy-eight people were killed, mostly young women with Irish names. The original memorial for the mass grave, which had worn down after fifty years, was replaced with a five-ton granite monument in 1912 that lists the names of all the dead as best as could be ascertained.

In the aftermath, a lengthy blame game played out. Symington was suspected of sabotage by some and fought to clear his name. A jury impaneled immediately by coroner John McClung found nearly all parties culpable. The majority opinion was that Alexander McBride and his assistant, James Thorpe, were found to have committed "gross neglect"; Symington and his lieutenants were found to have contributed to the accident through "neglect." Some jurors, however, placed the blame solely on McBride. Despite the fact that this civilian jury had no authority over military officers, Symington insisted on a military tribunal, which cleared him but not McBride. However, McBride kept his job while Symington was retired, a vindication of sorts. McBride, experienced as a barrel maker, blamed the spilled powder on the Du Pont Company's practice of reusing the wooden powder barrels, which resulted in loose lids and spilled powder. Workers had complained that the new stone road was too hard and liable to spark from horseshoes or iron wheels. McBride had ordered that a mixture of woodchips, sawdust and cinders be spread on the paving stones to reduce the risk of sparks, but Symington countermanded this order, and this precaution was swept away.

The Allegheny Arsenal explosion is frequently referred to as "Pittsburgh's worst day during the Civil War," but outside Pittsburgh, it was overshadowed by news of the Civil War's deadliest day of fighting: the Battle of Antietam. One thousand local residents petitioned Congress for $30,000 in compensation for victims' families but were denied. The site of the disaster is now the Arsenal Middle School, the adjacent green space of Arsenal Park and, across Butler Street, the warehouses that stretch to the Allegheny River. One of the original powder magazines from 1814 survives to this day and is used for Parks Department storage.

The Fenian Connection

We are the Fenian Brotherhood, skilled in the arts of war,
And we're going to fight for Ireland, the land we adore,
Many battles we have won, along with the boys in blue,
And we'll go and capture Canada, for we've nothing else to do.
—*Fenian soldier's song*

The ink was scarcely dry on Robert E. Lee's surrender at Appomattox when the Irish Civil War veterans known as Fenians set in motion their plans to invade Canada—yes, Canada. America has invaded so many countries it's difficult to keep track, but "we" have invaded Canada two and a half times: during the Revolutionary War, during the War of 1812 and after the Civil War. For the record, Confederate soldiers based in Canada had raided St. Albans, Vermont, during the Civil War, setting a precedent of sorts. This action, along with the British construction of the Confederate warship *Alabama*, was viewed as an example of Britain permitting or encouraging violations of its declared neutrality during the war. At the time when the Fenians were preparing to attack Canada, the administration of President Andrew Johnson was seeking reparations from England for violating neutrality, including $15 million in compensation for damages, mostly inflicted by the *Alabama*. Consequently, the U.S. government was not inclined to intervene early in Fenian plans to take part of Canada on behalf of Ireland. Instead, the prospect of U.S.-based Fenian invasions into British Canada was a bargaining chip in negotiations over reparations. It is said that the Fenian "president," William Randall Roberts, met with President Johnson, who agreed to "recognize the established facts," a curious turn of phrase possibly implying a repeat of the Texas land grab, where American citizens (and a few Mexicans) claimed independence from Mexico in an action not officially sanctioned by the U.S. government. In other words, the Fenians were given the impression that if they could establish a territory for themselves at the expense of the British, the United States would legitimize that "fact."

The Fenians, or Irish Republican Brotherhood (IRB), were a secret society that sought to eventually establish a free Ireland by military action, although they also had diplomatic strategies for achieving Irish independence through U.S. pressure on Britain. Nonetheless, all approaches were contingent on valiant fighting in the effort to preserve the Union. Charles McKenna makes no mention of Fenians or Fenianism in his letters, and it appears that they were a subdued presence in the 155th Pennsylvania Volunteers. However, the Fenian presence was clearly evident in Meagher's Irish Brigade. Fenians had their own patriotic songs, symbols such as the golden harp and secret initiation rituals. Some Irish former Confederate soldiers also participated in the Fenian raids, along with five hundred Mohawk Indians and one hundred African American veterans of the Union army.

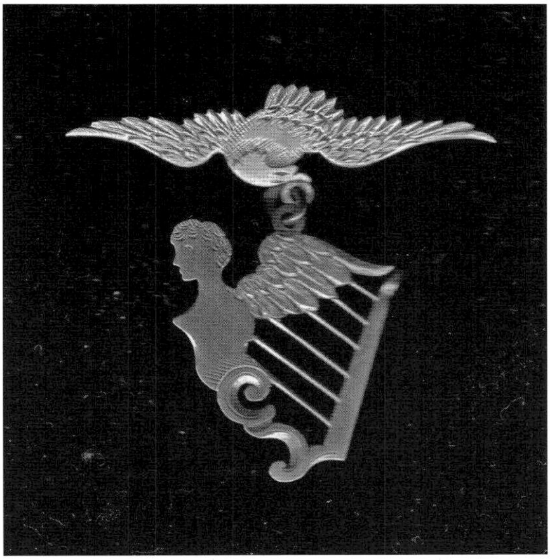

The Maltese Cross with Fenian Harp awarded to Colonel Bonbright. *Courtesy of Michael Kraus.*

As is typical with things Irish, there was some sharp disagreement over who was in charge and how to proceed. At a rancorous convention of the IRB Senate during October 1865 in New York, the dictatorial John O'Mahoney was toppled from his leadership post, and William Randall Roberts replaced him as chief executive, or president, of the senate. Ultimately, Major General "Fighting Tom" Sweeny, a veteran of both the Mexican and Civil Wars, was appointed secretary of war for the Fenians.

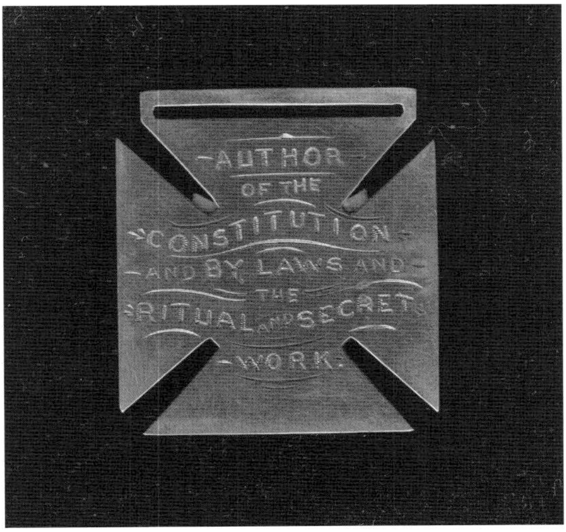

A Fenian inscription on the reverse of Bonbright's Maltese Cross. *Courtesy of Michael Kraus.*

Sweeny's plan for a three-pronged assault on Canada was approved in Pittsburgh during a meeting of the IRB Senate on February 19, 1866. In

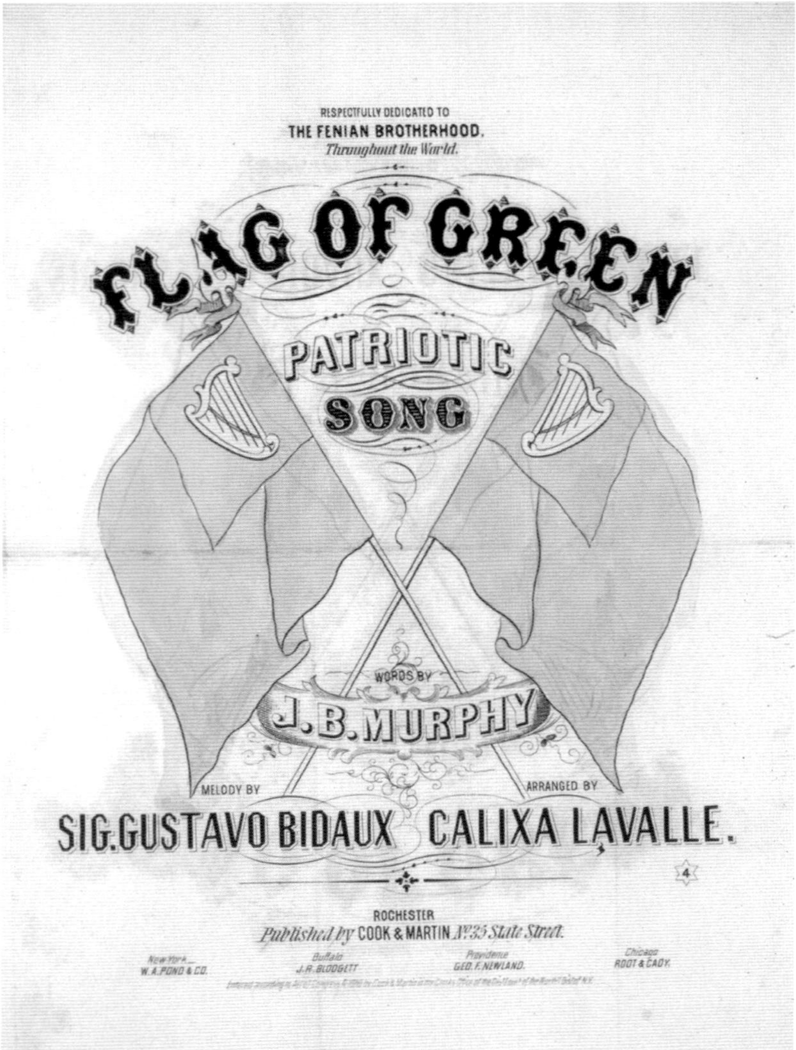

A Fenian patriotic song from 1866. *Courtesy of the Library of Congress.*

fact, Pittsburgh was a major recruitment center for the planned invasion, and the sale of Irish bonds raised a considerable amount of money. A gunboat was purchased in Pittsburgh, along with arms and ammunition. Sweeny was successful in purchasing weapons from U.S. arsenals, including four thousand muskets from Bridesburg, Pennsylvania, and two million rounds of ammunition from government stores in New York. The actual plan was quite ambitious and hinged on support from discontented Irishmen and French Canadians, but it must be remembered that the masterminds were not idle drunks in a barroom but experienced veterans and leaders fresh from the Civil War. It should also be noted that this time marks the earliest occurrence of the term Irish Republican Army (IRA). The original plan called for two diversionary threats to Toronto—a force launched from Chicago and Cleveland and another force crossing from Buffalo. The real threat to British control over Canada was supposed to be an assault on Montreal with over sixteen thousand men under Brigadier General Samuel P. Spear.

The invasion did not unfold as planned because a disgruntled O'Mahoney, hoping to regain control of the IRB, launched his own attack on New Brunswick. Betrayed by informers, the Fenians were quickly defeated. However, the British mistook this incident for the main raid and thought the threat was over. The bigger problem for the IRB was that O'Mahoney's actions spurred them to strike earlier than they had anticipated, and they were not able to follow Sweeny's original plan of attacking in winter and crossing into Canada over ice.

Trainloads of Irish veterans discreetly converged on Buffalo, New York, from Pittsburgh and other locales, along with weapons, some of which were smuggled into Canada and cached. Illness and logistical problems caused command of this force to fall upon John O'Neill of County Monaghan, and it is estimated that about one thousand men were able to assemble at Buffalo. Nonetheless, O'Neill proceeded according to plan, but he crossed the Niagara River with only eight hundred men on June 1, 1866. At first, his forces achieved several minor victories. Some accounts claim that O'Neill lost both the element of surprise and momentum by resting his men, but other narratives suggest that he was following a prudent procedure of constructing secure positions while awaiting reinforcement. In Chicago, Brigadier Charles Tevis made excuses, delayed and never attempted to enter Canada. Meanwhile, Ulysses S. Grant closed the border at Buffalo, preventing four thousand troops under Colonel Sherwin from reinforcing O'Neill. Ultimately, O'Neill's forces were surrounded by five thousand British troops and surrendered. Harsh sentences were given but later rescinded. At the same time, ten thousand militiamen and three warships prevented Spears's force from approaching Montreal, and there was no rising of the Irish there. Sweeny was briefly arrested but then continued to serve, without demotion, in the U.S. Army until 1870—an excellent illustration of official U.S ambiguity in the entire affair.

In hindsight, it appears that the Johnson administration used the threat of Fenian raids as a bargaining chip against the British, while the U.S.

military simultaneously undermined the Fenians at every turn, to the point of allowing the British to cross the border to pursue and kill Fenians in Vermont. On June 6, President Johnson, having received the long-sought $15 million in reparations, agreed in turn to enforce neutrality laws. The Fenian movement imploded not long after the Civil War, but many of its people and objectives became part of a new organization, Clan na Gael, which still exists today, albeit with greatly reduced numbers. O'Neill made two more unsuccessful attempts at undermining the English speakers' domination of Canada before retiring to what is now O'Neill, Nebraska. Few people remember that Pittsburgh was where an invasion of Canada was planned and launched. The lasting outcome of the Fenian invasions was the hasty creation of the Dominion of Canada, a federation that went into effect the year after O'Neill and his men crossed the Niagara River.

Part IV

IRISH IN THE MILLS AND MINES OF THE STEEL CITY, 1866–1914

To outsiders, the continuing entreaties of the Irish for famine relief may have become wearisome, but in many places, the situation was little improved from the starvation days of the 1840s. High rents and wet weather, coupled with a lengthy worldwide economic recession from 1873 to 1879, again made for desperate tenant farmers. The Irish American communities were the perennial source of fundraising for all sorts of schemes to save the mother country, and there were the inevitable rascals who diverted money inappropriately. This had been one of the contentions that split Fenianism—that O'Mahoney was misallocating funds. The history of Charles Stuart Parnell, agitation for home rule and the Land League in Ireland are far too complex to delve into here, but it should be noted that after the failed Canadian adventures, many Fenians chose to support the political reforms advocated by the Land League. The league organized resistance to evictions, fought for reductions in rents and aided the work of relief agencies. Rent strikes—that is, community-wide refusals to pay rent—were an effective strategy, but during the "land war," evictions and violence were commonplace. One goal of the Land League was to establish an equitable system that would allow tenants to buy land, and by 1905, some progress had been made in this regard.

Parnell and his entourage visited Pittsburgh in February 1880. Subsequently, many Irish Pittsburghers, including Charles McKenna, supported land reform schemes, and nearly every ward and parish hosted a Land League chapter. The largest Land League chapter in Pittsburgh was

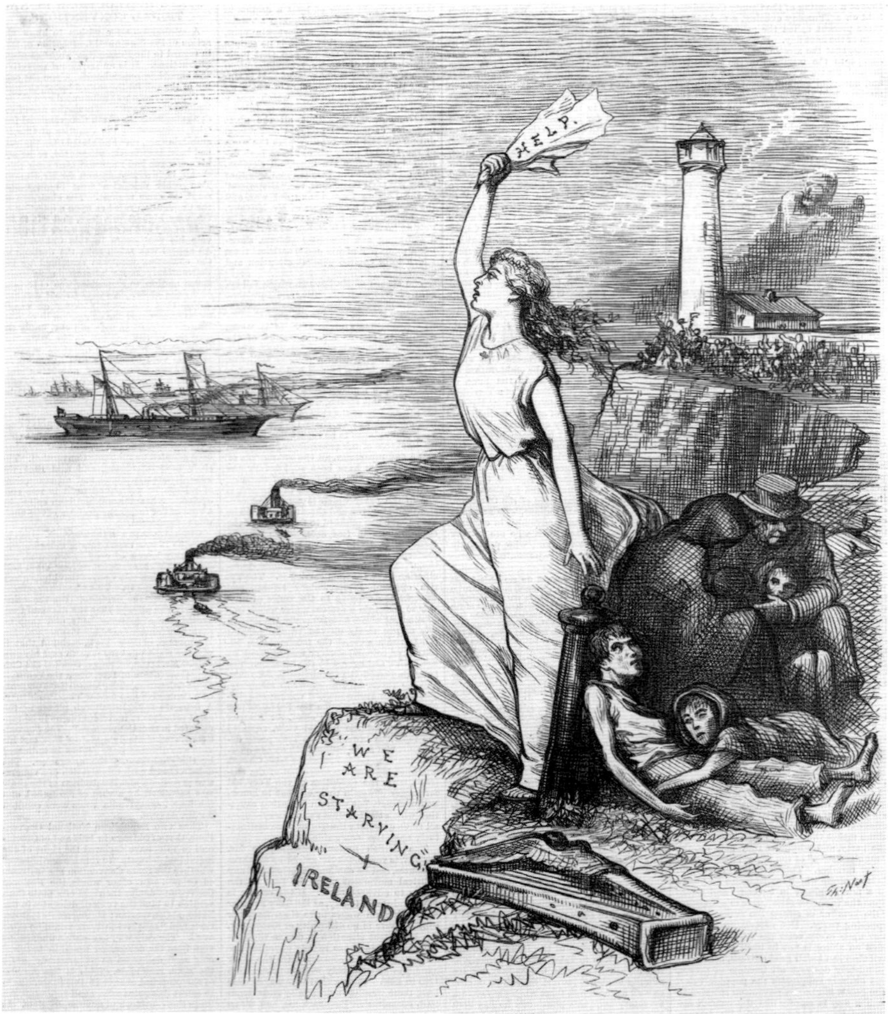

Harper's Weekly cover on starving Ireland, October 19, 1881. *Courtesy of the Library of Congress.*

that of St. Malachy's Church in West Pittsburgh; 80 percent of its members were ironworkers in the mills across the river from the Point. By 1882, a year's worth of small contributions by St. Malachy's members, ranging from twenty-five cents to $1, had raised nearly $800. The Robert Emmet Chapter of Lawrenceville included shopkeepers in addition to millworkers. Proponents of the Land League did not advocate armed insurrection; nonetheless, many Clan na Gael officers also held leadership positions in

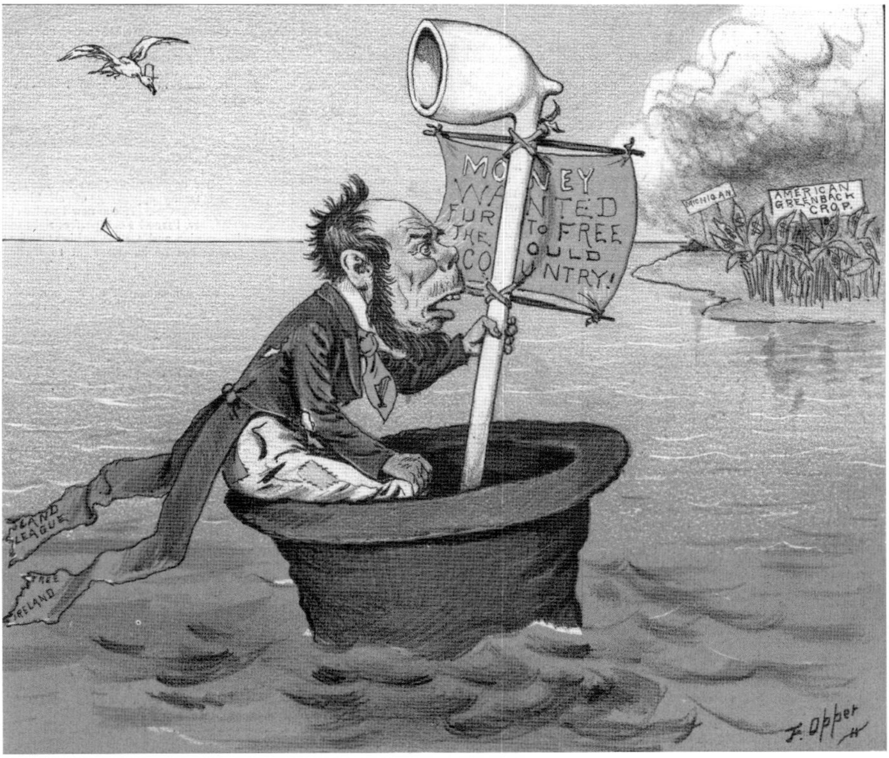

Puck magazine cover satirizing O'Connor's American fundraising, February 2, 1880. *Courtesy of the Library of Congress.*

Land League chapters. In 1881, the fundraising T.P. O'Connor of the Land League was caricatured on the cover of *Puck* magazine in rags, with ape-like features, navigating to American shores in a top hat labeled "O'Connor's Charity Craft," seeking the "American Greenback Crop" and proclaiming, "Wonst more, me byes, for Ould Oirland—the land of divilment and distress [*sic*]." Such mockery did not prevent Pittsburgh's Irish community—with both a rising moneyed middle class and a large number of workers willing to spare a mite—from becoming a perennial fundraising stop for Irish leaders.

Irishmen did not specialize in any one particular industry. As labor historian David Montgomery has noted, "The Irish were everywhere and into everything." The Irish in the American steel industry were like leavening in bread; they were important well beyond their numbers. As leaders of unionism in steel and other workplaces, they ranged in political belief from Communist and/or anarchist to conservative strains of Catholicism. It must be noted that the Irish have a long and mixed history of both supporting the church and defying its authority, although outsiders readily assume some sort of monolithic cohesion. The Irish had arrived early and often, and their institutions, including the Catholic Church, set the tone for the experiences of future waves of immigrants. Although many moved into foreman positions, their ability to speak English also enabled them to express the aspirations of their co-workers, who were increasingly Slavic speakers from Eastern Europe. The shifting fortunes of the Austro-Hungarian Empire and the Ottoman Empire made it difficult to describe from where, exactly, many of these immigrants originated. Pittsburghers, displaying the American tendency toward both xenophobia and ignorance in things geographic, frequently labeled all Eastern Europeans "Huns" or "Hungarians." On some occasions, Eastern Europeans served as strikebreakers, while at other times, as we shall see, they bore the brunt of the battle for fair working conditions.

Compared to the daughters of other immigrant groups in Pittsburgh, single Irish women were far more likely to work as live-in servants. This was undoubtedly due to a mixture of cultural mores and economic necessity. The only other ethnic group with a similar tolerance for allowing young women to live apart from family was African Americans. There was, however, one important distinction between the two groups concerning the practice of employment as live-in servants: young Irish women handed over their earnings to support the rest of their families, while African American servants typically saved to start families of their own. Stereotypes of "Brigit the Maid" and the gorilla-like "Brigit the Bruiser" were commonplace until the Irish won another fierce battle to put an end to these offensive practices in the twentieth century. In this era, *Puck* also lampooned the Irishman's penchant for labor agitation in a lighthearted and less offensive manner.

At this juncture, the Irish were making inroads into politics as well. One explanation commonly given for rapid entry of the Irish into politics is that most of them saw America as their country because they were never going back to Ireland, where friends and family often held "American funerals" for departing loved ones they would never see again. No political story from any major city from this era would be complete without instances of brazen corruption, and Pittsburgh does not disappoint in this regard. A case in point would be the McGee-Flinn machine. William Flinn's Irish parents emigrated from Manchester, England, in 1851 and settled in the Hill District. His father, John Flinn, established a small contracting business that assuredly influenced

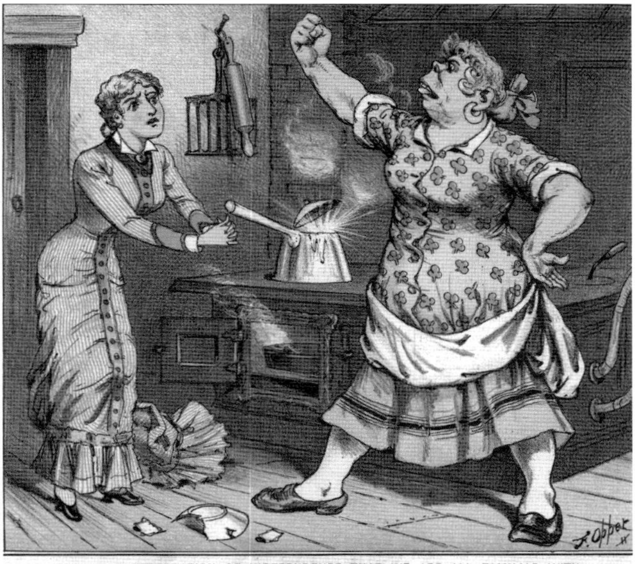

THE IRISH DECLARATION OF INDEPENDENCE THAT WE ARE ALL FAMILIAR WITH.

Puck magazine cover with the typical "Bridget the Bruiser" caricature, May 9, 1883. *Courtesy of the Library of Congress.*

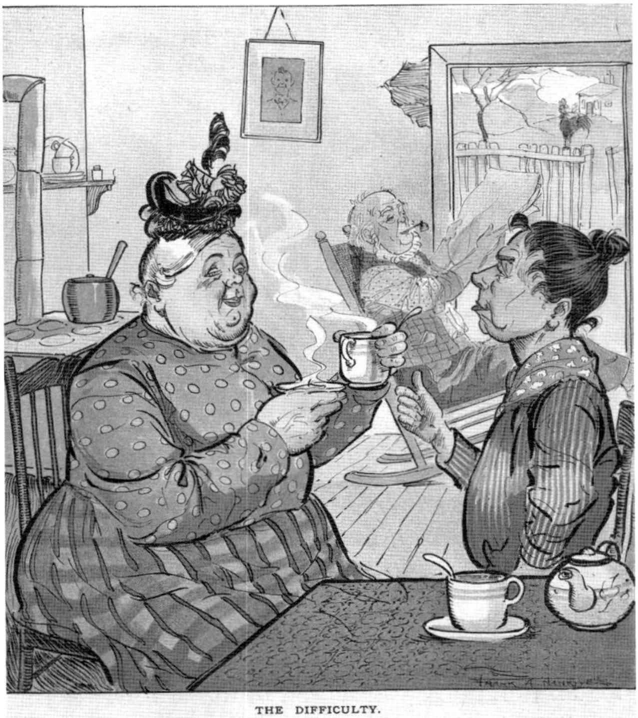

THE DIFFICULTY.

MRS. KELLY.—Does your husband get good pay, Mrs. Rooney?
MRS. ROONEY.—Well, he would, Mrs. Kelly, ef ut was n't fer shtriking so often fer *better* pay.

Puck magazine with the caption: "Mrs. Kelley.—'Does your husband get good pay, Mrs. Rooney?' Mrs. Rooney.—'Well he would Mrs. Kelly, ef ut was n't fer shtriking so often for *better* pay.'" December 17, 1902. *Courtesy of the Library of Congress.*

William's future calling as a contractor. Flinn, who dropped out of public school at age nine, was educated in the streets of Pittsburgh, delivering newspapers, shining shoes and apprenticing as a steamfitter. He started in the Republican Party as a ward boss and rapidly rose in the ranks, partnering with Christopher Magee, the city's Republican Party political boss. In 1877, Flinn was elected to represent the Pittsburgh area in the Pennsylvania State House, and in 1882, he was appointed chairman of the executive committee of the Pittsburgh Republican Party. In 1890, he was elected to the Pennsylvania State Senate, where he pressed for the Good Roads Act, which passed in 1895.

However, in classic Pennsylvania fashion, Flinn was not above conflict of interest. His large-scale contracting firm, Booth and Flinn, proved highly profitable. He used his political connections, manipulated or rigged the "lowest responsible bidder" process and garnered most of the large construction and paving contracts in Pittsburgh and western Pennsylvania. His firm built infrastructure that stands today, including the Liberty, Wabash and Armstrong Tunnels in Pittsburgh, as well as streets, trolley lines and bridges. Disgruntled competitors made allegations of graft and corruption, and Flinn's wings were eventually trimmed when reformers passed legislation to reduce corruption and kickbacks. Despite his self-serving record, Flinn is memorialized by a stretch of Route 8 just north of Pittsburgh, although his name is persistently misspelled as "Flynn."

It was not until the 1870s that Pittsburgh's Catholic community was able to successfully establish the college that is now Duquesne University. Father John Bernard Strub, a refugee from Otto van Bismarck's newly unified Germany, was permitted to set up a college, although the Diocese of Pittsburgh could not provide land, buildings or money. The original school, located above a bakery on Wylie Avenue in the lower Hill District, opened on October 1, 1878. Strub soon departed, and a series of Irish priests took over. Despite low enrollment, in 1882 the Pittsburgh Catholic College received its charter from the State of Pennsylvania. For the first eight years, students were distracted by the smell of baking bread that filled their school building. Finally, Father William Patrick Power was able to purchase property on the bluff above the Monongahela River from the heirs of Dr. A.G. Walter. However, Power had to resort to using a third-party buyer because Walter's heirs would not sell to a Catholic institution. On this site, the building known today as "Old Main" was constructed, a process that required leveling the hilltop, removing rock and clay and setting up a brickyard where the priests themselves formed the clay into bricks. From the onset, these European priests were keenly aware that Americans valued practical education and the ability to speak English, which helps explain why the college survived when three-quarters of all Catholic colleges founded before 1900 failed.

In the Barroom

I'm a celebrated workingman, my duties I don't shirk
I can cut more coal than any man from Pittsburgh to New York
It's a holy terrogation, boys, how I get through my work
While I'm seated at my glory in the barroom.

—*Ed Foley*

It is indeed a good question how miners and millworkers got anything done if they drank so much. The hard work of miners and millworkers in western Pennsylvania is the stuff of legend and textbooks; less remembered are their bragging skills. The Irish were masters of both. The notion of a prodigiously strong worker of limitless productivity has always resonated with Pittsburgh audiences, as exemplified in the better-known tales of John Henry and Joe Magarac. However, such working-class stories must be approached carefully, as they contain multiple layers of meaning and often function as cautionary tales. "The Celebrated Working Man," for example, was a clever commentary on a hard-drinking and hardworking culture. The song was originally composed by an Irish Pennsylvanian miner, Ed Foley, but has traveled extensively since. The lyrics were rife with self-irony about barroom bragging rights, but the barroom boasting had substance behind it in the outside world, where western Pennsylvania's mines and mills fed the world's voracious appetite for steel and glass. Ed Foley, also known as the "Irish minstrel boy," was reported to have first performed the song at a niece's wedding in 1892. Since then, it has followed a divergent and transnational path. Jim Roberts, an anarchist miner from Kentucky, carried the song to the mining towns of Durham in northern England sometime around the First World War. With the inevitable modifications, including the addition of the refrain "in the barroom," the song became firmly ensconced in English working-class tradition. Meanwhile, the song also remained part of the tradition in its native Pennsylvania, where it was later collected by Michael F. Barry.

Folklorist George Korson has depicted the Welsh and Irish songwriters of the coalfields as "miner bards…brothers of the Celtic wandering minstrels of old, vagabonds with a distaste for the mining craft," and yet, a strong sense of pride in strength and skill is evident in some ballads. In the era before automation was fully developed, effectively de-skilling much of the work, many workers were successively unionized on a craft basis, as opposed to an industry-wide basis. Workingmen's songs—ostensibly about hardship and resistance—often take Welsh and Irish forms, such as the hymn and the comic ballad, that appear to foreground the celebratory in a manner that undermines the protest. The satirical voice, in turn, undercuts the voice of celebration. Consequently, the lyrics to "The Celebrated Working Man" are conflicted and contradictory, with a strong whiff of the self-referential. Gerald Porter has pointed out that, in Ireland, narrative has often lacked the sequential character familiar to audiences of other European ballads. Likewise, "The Celebrated Working Man" is not a linear story but a series of disconnected boasts that ultimately concludes in the apparent context of the song itself—that is, in the smoke-filled barroom:

And now my song is o'er and I don't have any other
For heaven's sake don't fire no more or else we'll surely smother
The landlord would rather throw us out then go to the bother
Of putting up a ventilator in the barroom.

Outside the barroom, down in the working world, a miner's productivity depended on his assigned work area, called a "room," and his pay was directly linked to how much he could hew out of the rock in twelve hours. The boss's favor meant the difference between working a "wet hole" and working a good room. A story goes that one evening, a mine boss chanced to pass by a tavern where he overheard one of his workers boasting of his superhuman capabilities for wresting coal from the earth. The next morning, the boss apprehended the braggart, declaring, "Paddy, I bet you're not as good at digging coal today as you imagined yourself to be in the barroom last night." Paddy, always quick with a retort, replied, "I would be, if you could give me the same room I had last night." Songs should always be considered in their wider social context; viewed in this light, "The Celebrated Working Man" may also be a cautionary tale about bragging too much in the barroom. Alternatively, the song could be read as a highly roundabout criticism of poor working conditions, coupled with commentary on the ill-ventilated drinking environment.

In the 1870s, a third of Pittsburgh's ubiquitous licensed saloons were run by Irish proprietors, but this count overlooks the multitude of illegal grogshops run by widows and other poor Irish immigrants who could never have afforded the seventy-five-dollar fee for a state license. Like the mines and mills, the saloons were no place for a lady, although children and women were frequently expected to run beer back to the men in their rooms or shanties. This practice was known as "rushing the growler," perhaps after the gurgling sound of fresh-tapped beer in a tin can or bucket or, alternately, after a medieval measure of eight pints. In May 1885, *Puck* magazine disapprovingly commented on the practice: "The old, old story. The happy home, loving parents, the growler, the fall and ruin." Moralistic commentators, who often had an anti-immigrant bias, viewed growler-rushing as the first step down a slippery slope toward self-destruction, destitution and dependence on alms.

In an era that marked the height of laissez-faire capitalism, governmental intervention in family life was limited to the police, judges and aldermen; social welfare programs were nonexistent. Agents of the Humane Society, which sought to protect children from neglect or abuse by their caretakers, prowled the poorer districts looking for cases. Often these agents were Irish, albeit middle class, or "lace curtain Irish." These agents were used to a private home life that was utterly lacking in the packed slums where neighbors heard everything through thin walls. Humane Society agents usually found injury and dire poverty to be the causes of distress, but the role of alcoholism was frequently noted. In neglectful cases, they threatened to remove children, and through fear they influenced entire neighbourhoods by their very presence. For instance, S.J. Kleinbergh has recounted in *The Shadow of the Mills* how Mr. O'Brien, a Humane Society agent, could parade family trouble before neighbors. Investigating possible child neglect by Mrs. O'Connors, a widowed shopkeeper, O'Brien revealed himself only after interviewing neighbours, telling her that if she did not stop drinking and care for her children, he would "feel obliged to take the children from her." In another instance, however, O'Brien's attempt to collect witnesses failed because the neighbors themselves were "drunk as oysters."

Drinking, like all other social activities, was clearly stratified in Pittsburgh's Irish community. Successful "lace curtain" Irishmen (and it was always men) blended in at downtown Pittsburgh's "gilded saloons" and the private clubrooms of swank hotels, meeting with colleagues at lunchtime or after work. Careers in finance, contracting and politics invariably required a physical and cultural closeness to city hall. For these men, drinking in the right places indicated upward mobility and success. This was the milieu in which Irish Catholics like Charles and Bernard McKenna rose to eminence in Pittsburgh politics.

For the tired millworker or glassblower, the saloon was more than a respite from otherwise incessant work. Skilled workers, such as iron and glassworkers, frequented the saloons near the mills, attempting to rehydrate themselves. This was undoubtedly safer than drinking the untreated water pumped into the mills from rivers filled with all manner of industrial byproducts and sewage. Whiskey was commonly believed by ironworkers to strengthen their constitution; however, drinking by workers was a common reason given by mill owners for injuries and deaths on the job—and a convenient excuse to avoid implementing a safer workplace and paying compensation to injured workers or widows.

Laborers at the bottom of the wage scale, along with a host of ne'er-do-wells, frequented the illegal drinking establishments or "kitchen barrooms," hiding in boarding rooms, grocery stores, cellars and attics. The dodgy grogshops that lined the riverbanks featured a culture of drinking and fighting, which defined manhood for those too poor and transient to marry. The lethal ferocity of binge-drinking lower-class Irish Pittsburgh was alarming, even for Irishmen, as this passage from a letter by teamster William Murphy attests:

> *The people here can far beat your country* [Ireland] *killing one another. The people here think as little of killing others as you would of killing the mice in a cornstack. Theirs* [sic] *no such thing as men fighting here as they would about a Saintfeld* [near Belfast] *fair for if ever you get into a fight here you must either kill or be killed. Men are permitted to carry pistols and large knives which they use instead of fighting with their fists.*

These murderous brawls were a staple of Pittsburgh's news reporting, and they often took on dimensions of ethnic conflict as well. A prominent example in September 1886 was a series of fights between Italians and Irishmen that culminated in a riotous home invasion with deaths on both sides. Clerical and political authorities were perpetually frustrated in their attempts to mitigate a crisis that was rooted in dire poverty in an era when government social services, including garbage pickup, were nonexistent. In the 1870s, two-thirds of all the Irish arrested for public intoxication were unskilled workers under the age of thirty.

The homes of skilled workers and laborers were cramped and dirty, and they could not afford the recreational amenities available to the middle class, such as the nickelodeon, even when they did speak English. The middle-class worldview, presented in magazines such as *People's Monthly*, advised women to keep a clean and pleasant house in order to encourage their men to stay home rather than squander the rewards of their hard work in saloons. This advice was absurd to the wives of millworkers or day laborers, who waged a futile war against the relentless airborne soot, grime and feces inevitably tracked in from outside their tight quarters.

The Magee-Flinn political machine preferred to remain in power and make money rather than lose elections by enforcing unpopular puritanical laws that restricted drinking. In the mid-1880s, a self-appointed Law and Order Society emerged in Pittsburgh that was part of a wider Law and Order League in America. The Law and Order Society crusaded against saloons and for enforcement of Pennsylvania's Blue Laws, which restricted sales, amusements and liquor on Sundays. The self-appointed Law and Order Society took action by submitting complaints over violations of existing laws in the courts. It also pushed for prohibition but had to settle instead for strict state licensing laws. Passed in 1887, Pennsylvania's new law reduced the number of county licenses for serving alcohol from 3,000 to 389 and city licences from 1,500 to 223.

In Pittsburgh, the league accomplished 325 convictions for violating the law in the first six months after its passage. However, enforcement was uneven and ineffectual, and the law was widely flouted. At this time, the term "speakeasy" may have first originated (or at least became popular) in the McKeesport saloon of Kate Hester, when she admonished her patrons to quiet down so as not to draw the attention of the police or neighbors. Songs like "Soho on a Saturday Night" were comic satires of attempts to legislate morality and sobriety for the millworkers in this rough-and-tumble uptown neighborhood:

The men with the bottles, their wives with a can,
And young girls go prowlin' a-round like a man…
And the new li-cence plan, it ain't worth a damn
In soho on Sat-ur-day night.

To be fair, the Law and Order League claimed that it "never proposed to reform anyone, but solely to enforce the law and leave the reformation of the inmates to those societies whose particular province it may be." In any event, efforts to control saloon culture invariably met with little success, and the barrooms persisted as centers of musical, social and political life.

Many prohibitionists had strong anti-Catholic and anti-immigrant agendas. The Irish of Pittsburgh deeply resented the long history of British propaganda, Know-Nothing pamphleteering and vicious cartoons by Thomas Nast that portrayed them as incorrigible drunkards; therefore, they had their own public responses to the problem of alcoholism. The Catholic Total Abstinence Union was strong in Pittsburgh, led predominantly by immigrants and Americans of Irish descent, and drew its support from the middle classes. Another notable organization connected with unionism was the Young Men's Temperance Union (YMTU). Francis Murphy, a failed hotel and saloon owner turned Methodist preacher, conducted what has been described as the "greatest temperance revival ever known." On November 26, 1876, Murphy addressed a crowd of eight thousand people at Pittsburgh's opera house, and in 1877, a national organization was founded with its headquarters in Pittsburgh. Murphy's personal narrative of fall and redemption was his primary argument, and he shunned the political solutions put forth by prohibitionists. His style and message appealed to both skilled craftsmen and common laborers; a lack of self-righteousness or class prejudice enabled him to reach a working-class audience that was usually put off by the lectures of temperance preachers. The founders of Pittsburgh's craft unions had, from their inception, attempted to legislate against drunkenness on the job. Industrial unionism under Terence Powderly's Knights of Labor sought to include all members of the "producing classes"—except saloonkeepers, who were "devils imps," in Powderly's words. For Murphy, sobriety meant voluntary self-control rather than compulsory abstinence for all of society. Sobriety also made possible disciplined soldiers in the army of organized labor, while saloons were seen as breeding grounds for strikebreakers.

Life at the Point

While New York City had its notorious "Five Points" slum neighborhood, Pittsburgh had but one "Point" at the confluence of the Allegheny and Monongahela Rivers, but it was sufficiently squalid. The Point, originally the site of Fort Pitt and later a part of the young city, declined from a dirty rough-and-tumble frontier city to a miserable slum. Beginning in the 1850s, a new influx of Irish immigrants settled at the Point, which became known as "Little Ireland." Too close to the ever-flooding rivers and surrounded by

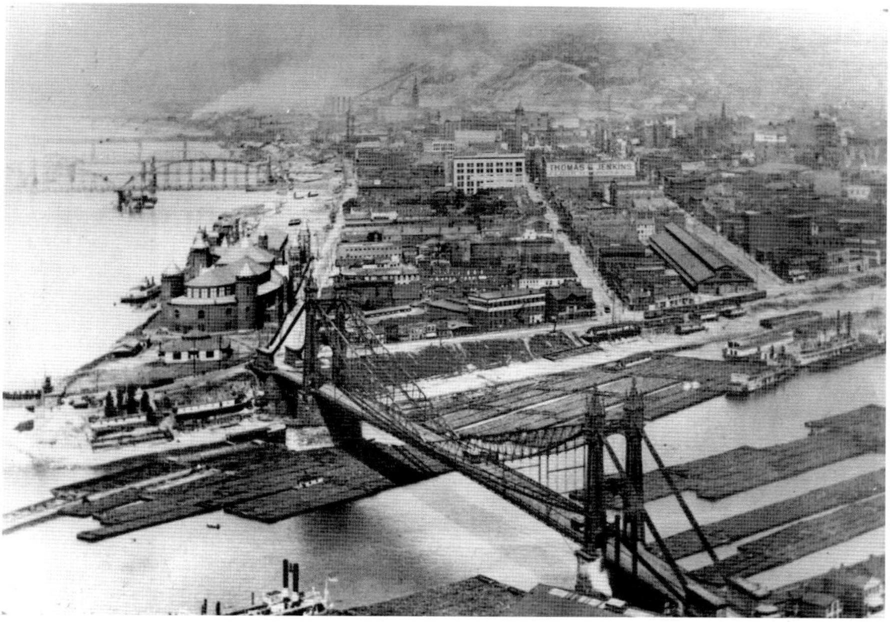

The Point from Mount Washington, late 1800s. *Courtesy of Carnegie Library of Pittsburgh, Oakland.*

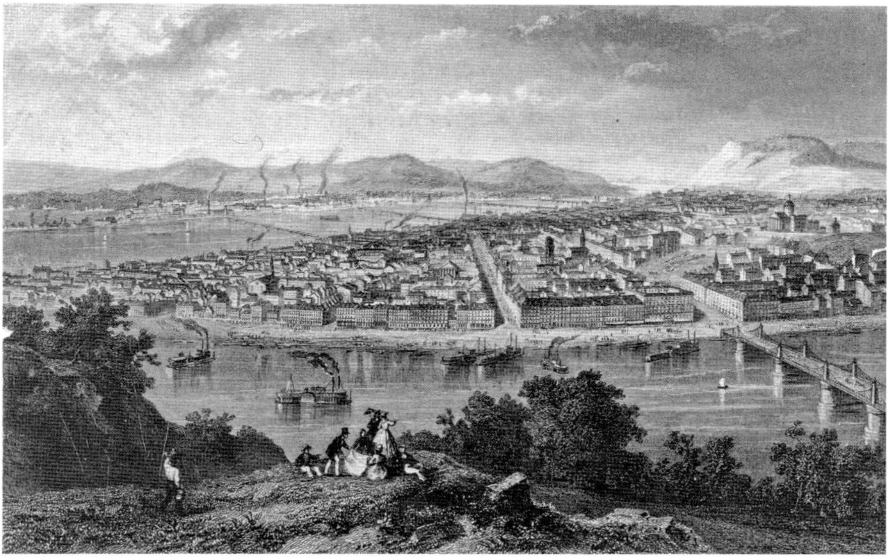

Pittsburgh from Mount Washington (Coal Hill), 1877. *Courtesy of Carnegie Library of Pittsburgh, Oakland.*

industrial development, the Point was eventually abandoned by its upper- and middle-class inhabitants. Through it all, the original Fort Pitt Block House remained as a dwelling rather than a fortification. One clear sign that the Point was becoming a low-rent district was the fact that the Fort Pitt Block House rent went down—from forty dollars monthly for the entire structure in 1836 to a mere five dollars for the top floor and four dollars for the lower floor in 1880.

The Point was a natural collection area for all sorts of vile effluvia, both human and industrial waste, because it was downhill from the rest of the city and there were no sewers. By 1876, the Point had become "the principal place of deposit for all kinds of filth and rubbish which has made it, without exception, the filthiest and most disagreeable locality within the limits of the city...the poorer classes, living in many cases in extreme poverty, and occupying the merest apologies for houses," according to the Fourth Annual Report of the Bureau of Industrial Statistics. In August 1877, cholera struck the Irish quarter, which ran along the Allegheny River from the Point up to Fifteenth Street. Most of the 984 deaths in this citywide outbreak were children.

Victor A. Walsh's study of the Point in the 1870s and '80s found that most of its residents hailed from Galway and Connemara in western Ireland. Not only did they not speak English, but they were also from parts of Ireland so remote that they were "untouched by the world of the Protestant ascendency" and its associated capitalism. Unlike a number of earlier and contemporary Irish immigrants, they were not skilled craftsmen, and they occupied the lowest rung of the wage scale as laborers. These immigrants did not attend Mass at the cathedral. They were dressed in rags, and in any event, they were more familiar with the village chapel or with visiting clerics holding Mass in thatched cottages. The cult of St. Brigit, readily tossed aside by many Irish immigrants, held sway a little longer among these newcomers from rural western Ireland. St. Mary's Church in the Point became the religious focal point of Little Ireland. Originally a mission for St. Paul's Cathedral that started in a small chapel in 1868, St. Mary's acquired the AME Methodist Episcopal Church on the corner of Third Avenue and Ferry Street in 1876. With the assistance of Reverend Morgan P. Sheedy, St. Mary of Mercy's School opened at 216 Penn Avenue in 1890, providing education for the immigrant children who became the next generation of Pittsburgh's Irish community.

The Fort Pitt Block House, the last remnant of the fort built in 1764 under Colonel Bouquet, was inhabited by Irish families for decades while the Point was a slum. It is difficult to precisely determine who lived there for

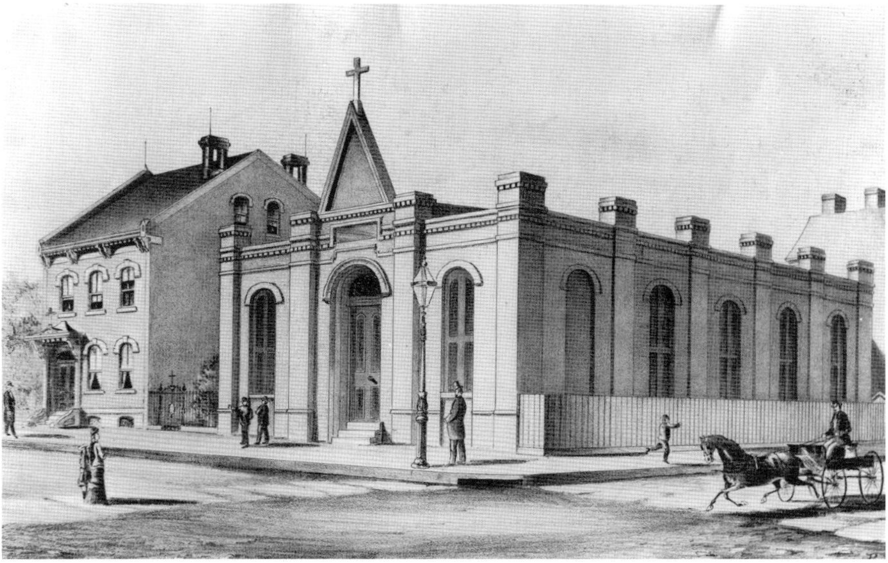

Above: St. Mary's Church in The Point. *Courtesy of the Catholic Historical Society.*

Right: St. Mary's School's first building. *Courtesy of the Catholic Historical Society.*

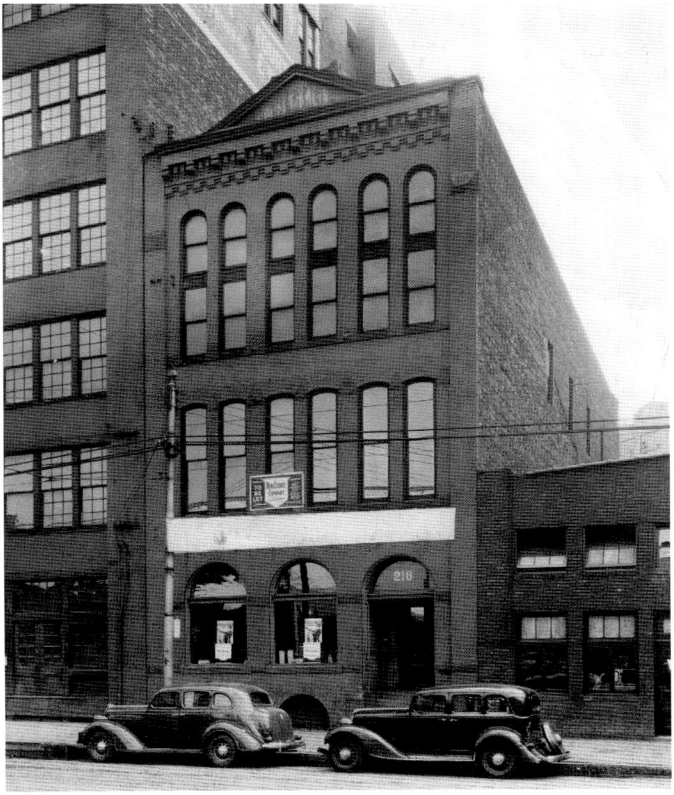

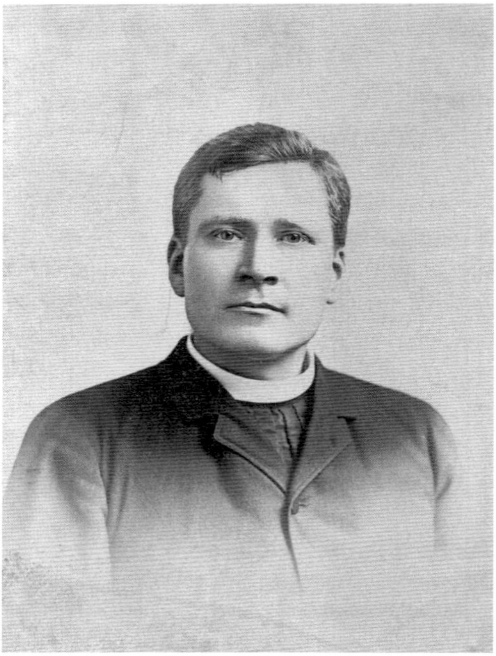

Reverend Morgan P. Sheedy. *Courtesy of the Catholic Historical Society.*

most of the nineteenth century, and there are conflicting or unsubstantiated claims about residents. Census records were not as precise then, and the first and second floors were apparently on different streets that underwent several name changes. In any case, this was a solidly Irish neighborhood, and typical estimates are that as many as twenty people in two extended households could have occupied a structure that is approximately the size of a small Cape Cod–style house. Some of the later Irish residents are known to us through interviews conducted by reporters and, later, scholars.

Best remembered is "Sibby Powers," an Irish widow, provenance unknown, who ran a small store from her downstairs apartment. The store consisted of three shelves placed in a window; in April 1894, the window display featured "five dried up ginger snaps" and "two little oranges perched on antiquated teacups," according to the *Pittsburgh Post*, along with cakes, stick candy, peppermint drops and chewing gum. Her extensive inventory included a few practical items that might be needed in a hurry—small knives, thread and hairpins. The *Post* reporter noted that the only other items in the first floor were a bed, stove and boxes. A widow for about twenty-five years by this time, Powers (who appears to be listed as Mrs. Flaherty in census records) raised most of her four-dollar rent from the store. There is no record of this particular widow being charged with conducting business on the Sabbath. Many former Point residents, including future Irish mayor David Lawrence, fondly remembered Powers and her candy, and today's Fort Pitt Block House museum includes a replica of the store. Two widows and their families also lived upstairs until the Daughters of the American Revolution (DAR) began their efforts to restore the property and evicted all tenants in 1894.

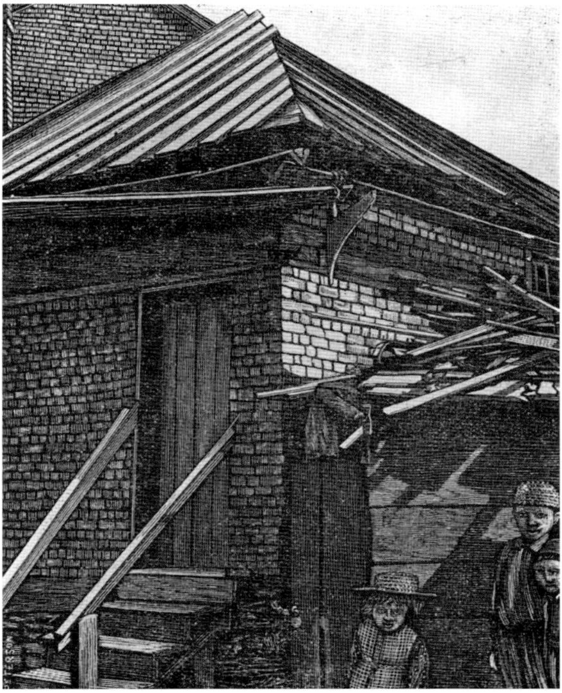

Right: Fort Pitt Block House as a slum, 1888. *From* "Flem's" Views of Old Pittsburgh.

Below: The blockhouse and tenants, 1890. *Courtesy of Carnegie Library of Pittsburgh, Oakland.*

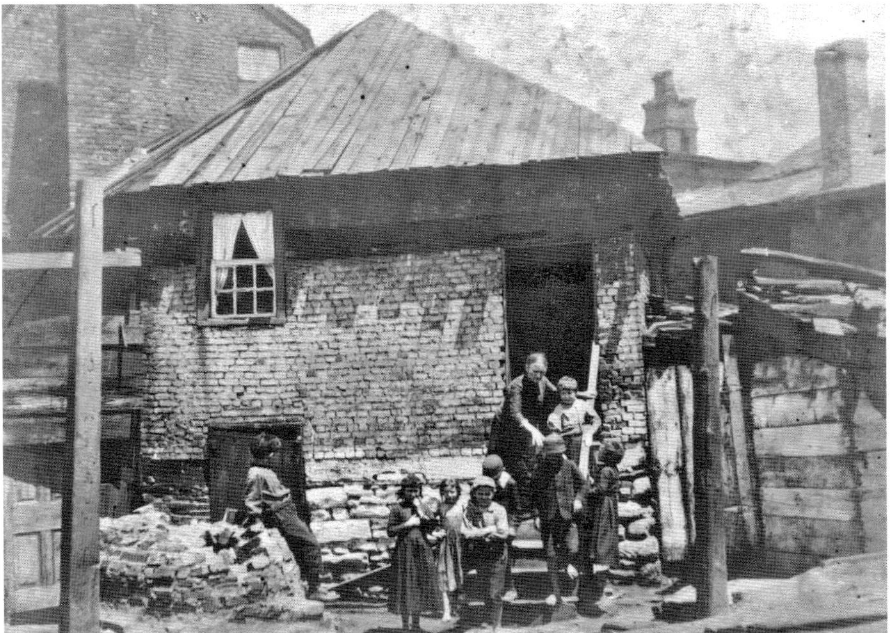

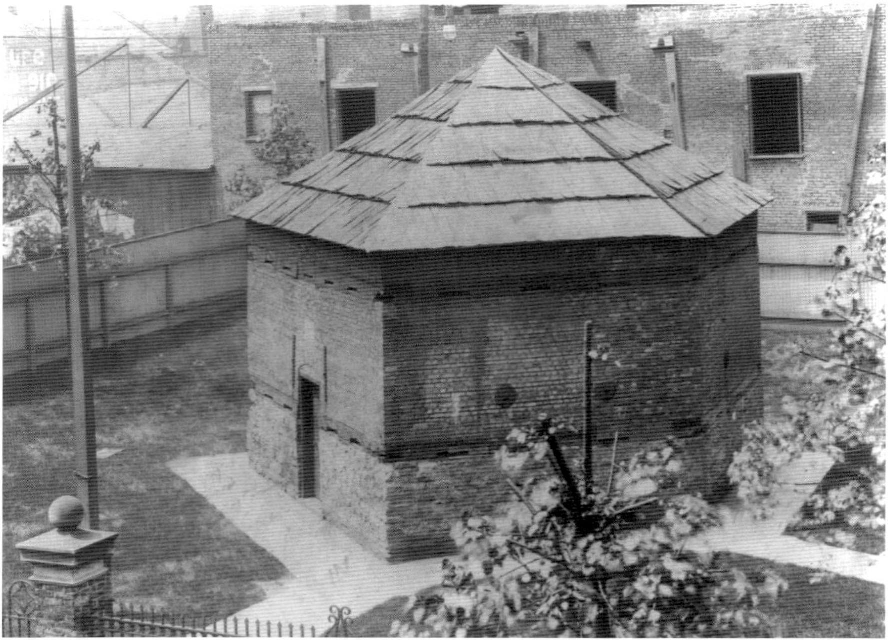

The Fort Pitt Block House during restoration, early 1900s. *Courtesy of the Library of Congress.*

During this era, the Point also featured twenty less reputable stores: the notorious cigar stores operated by unmarried women or widows that fronted for houses of prostitution. In 1887, the aforementioned Law and Order Society initiated a campaign to rid the city of prostitutes. The result was that they simply relocated across the river to Allegheny City, now North Side, and continued quietly to receive company, often renting rooms with private families. The Law and Order Society also harassed widows who sold liquor illegally or remained open on the Sabbath. This selective enforcement of the Blue Laws did not endear the Law and Order Society to the working class, and a writer for the *Commoner and Glass Worker* sharply noted that, while the mills remained open, an "old lady has committed the terrible crime of selling on Sunday. Arrest her quick in the interest of public peace and morality and add another to the list of persecuted cripples and orphans." No attempt at legislating morality ever cleaned up the Point, but the railroad companies acquired the land and cleared it for their rail yards, except for the Fort Pitt Block House, which the DAR preserved in an epic struggle.

Readers might well wonder how bad it was in Ireland and of the necessities that drove these people to live in the horrible slum at the Point.

Western Ireland, or Connaught, "hugged the Atlantic seaboard and differed appreciably from the rest of Ireland. Dominated by rain-soaked bogs, mountainous peninsulas, and rock-barren hills, much of this area…was uncultivable wasteland," in the words of Victor Walsh. Land was divided among sons, which led to a preponderance of "smallholders," or sustenance farmers who survived by cultivating potatoes on plots that diminished with each generation. This wave of immigrants who settled at the Point continued to speak Gaelic. They also differed from many earlier arrivals in their degree of wretched poverty, lack of skills suited to prospering in an industrial city and the extent to which they attempted to retain provincial loyalties in a new homeland where earlier Irish immigrants were beginning to forge a sense of national identity.

Dunbar's Mules

To the south and east of Pittsburgh, the Connellsville bed of the Pittsburgh coal seam runs for forty miles from Smithfield to Latrobe, between the Laurel and Chestnut Ridges. This coal was ideal for coking because it was almost pure carbon and there was no need to wash out impurities or remove slate. "Connellsville Coke" fed the mills that lined the three rivers and drove the great industrial machine of America. Near Connellsville, the Dunbar Furnace Company sourced its own coking coal from the Hill Farm Mine. Referring to themselves as "Dunbar's Mules," many Irishmen worked for long hours at low pay, hacking out and carting ore to the surface of the hill just west of Dunbar. One of the miners' greatest fears was firedamp, the methane gas that seeped out of the coal seams, forming scentless, invisible and highly explosive pockets.

On the morning of June 16, 1890, fifty-seven men set to work, thirty-one in the right heading of the mine and twenty-six in the left heading. Near the point where the headings split, a new shaft had been drilled recently, but it was not yet connected to the mine tunnels. The shaft had filled with a five-hundred-foot-high column of water, and when Patrick Kerwin accidentally broke through to the shaft with his pick, water surged through the hole at incredible pressure. Kerwin's assistant, David Hayes, entered the flooding left passage to warn the miners below, but he did not know that the rapid draining of water from the shaft had vacuumed methane gas out of the surrounding rock. His lamp ignited the gas, killing him. The twenty-six on

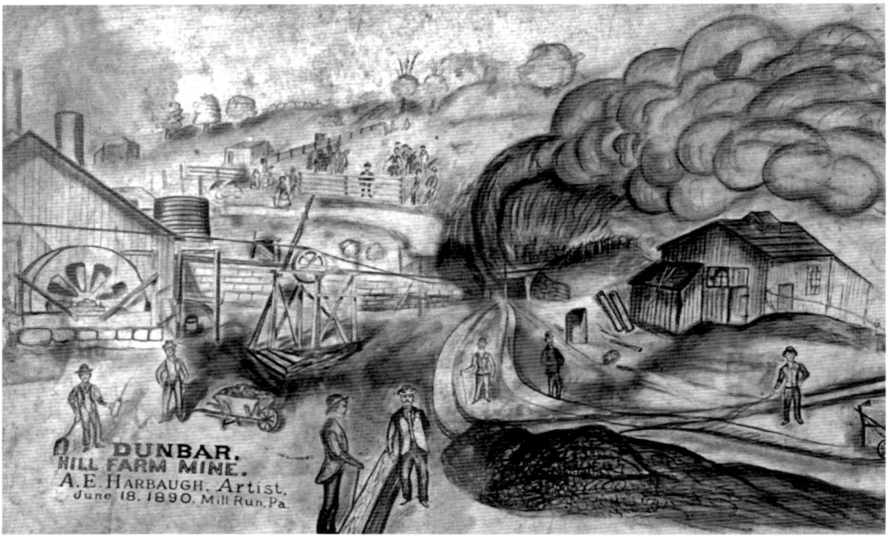

A sketch of the Dunbar mine disaster by eyewitness A.E. Harbaugh, "The Mountain Poet." *Courtesy of the Dunbar Historical Society.*

the left were alerted in time and scarcely managed to escape, along with Patrick Kerwin. The ensuing fire trapped all thirty-one men in the right heading. A black cloud of smoke began to loom over the mine, signaling to all that something below had gone very wrong.

Two hours later, the flames reached the surface and shot out, filling the sky with "clouds of fire" as the smoke ignited. Mining families and the entire community of Dunbar watched and waited for news, hoping to see loved ones in the blackened faces of the escaped miners. Thousands of people gathered at the mouth of the mine over the afternoon. "Neighbors gathered into each stricken home and while they comforted the living they prayed for the dead, and while they watched the fire they seemed to mentally bury their loved ones," noted a correspondent from the Frederick, Maryland *News*.

A force of about one hundred men made rescue attempts, but the flames were impassable, and an attempt at drilling another passage proved unsuccessful because their maps of the mine were inaccurate. Guards were then placed to prevent miners or distraught family members from entering the mine. McCleary, McCune, Bigley, Hays, Cahill and many other Irish names were among those of the missing. Sons commonly joined their fathers in the mines, learning the trade, and some families suffered a double blow; the Cope family lost both the Civil War veteran John Cope and his son, Andy

Cope. It took two years for the mine to burn and cool down before the bodies could be retrieved. The unfortunate miners had been suffocated, not burned, and their bodies devoured by rats. Identification required a bit of detective work; one man was identified by his pay stub, another by his pocket watch, still another by his shoes being on the wrong feet. The only positive outcomes of this accident—which nearly all parties agreed it was—were new safety regulations to the effect that no one else should be in a mine when a new shaft is opened.

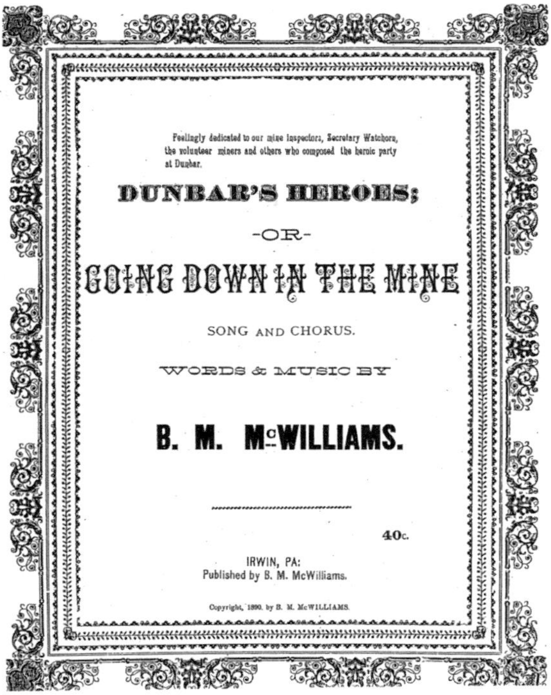

"Dunbar's Heroes" sheet music cover. *Courtesy of the Dunbar Historical Society.*

A contemporary song of tribute, "Dunbar's Heroes" by B.M. McWilliams, extolled the virtues of the rescue workers and is still performed in some musical circles today:

Going down in the darkness, the way lone and drear
The lamps burning dimly, too dimly to cheer
With unfaltering footsteps they cross the dark line
There are hearts brave and true going down in the mine…

How we cherish our heroes of land and of wave
The brave boys who perished our dear flag to save
But there's none that our hearts will more fondly enshrine
Than the lifesaving band that went down in the mine.

We readily commemorate those who risk their lives to defend America in time of war but quickly forget the brave men who attempt rescues in mines that are liable to collapse, flood or explode. This was one of many mining tragedies, and it was not the most fatal, but it is representative of the experiences of thousands of children of Eire who found themselves the subjects of "King Coal" in Pennsylvania.

An Irishtown once existed southeast of Dunbar, along what is now Irishtown Run, and many friends and relatives of the deceased miners no doubt lived there. Locals say that sometimes a "John Stone from Dublin," dressed in old-fashioned clothes and carrying a lantern, can be seen near two large rocks across the valley from a strip mine. He was supposedly killed when he was crushed between coal cars. Perhaps the spirit of Mr. Stone is compelled to warn others of the dangers of the coalfields and to encourage visitors to stay on the road because abandoned mine sites are treacherous

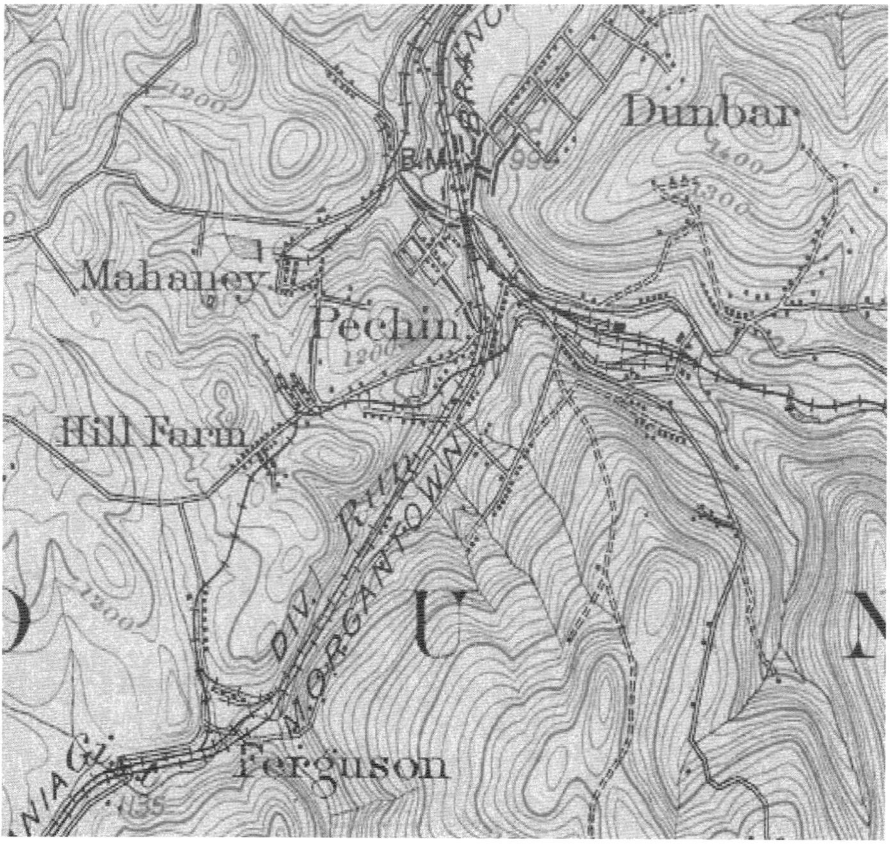

United States Geological Survey Map of Dunbar around 1900. Irishtown Run is in the lower right corner. *Courtesy of USGS.*

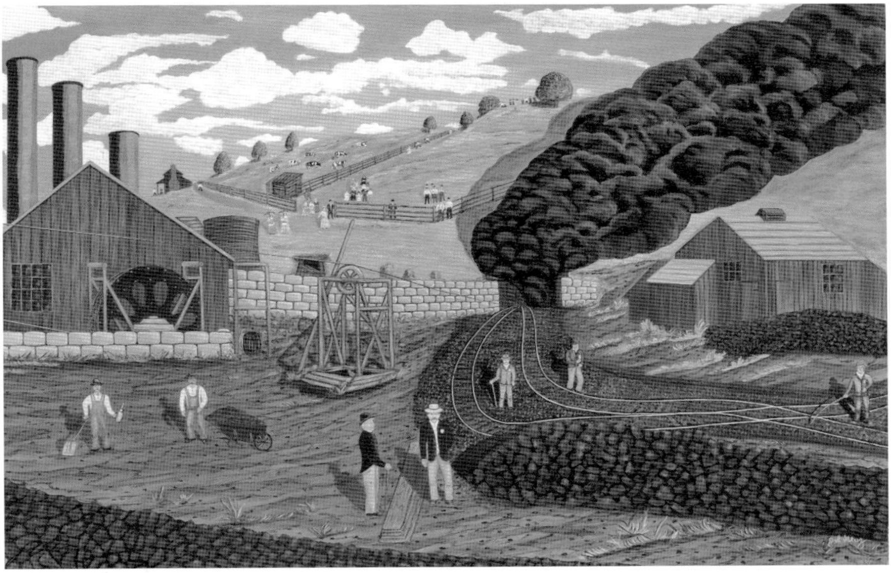

Painting of the Dunbar mine disaster by Steven Glutz. *Courtesy of Steven Glutz and the Dunbar Historical Society.*

places. His name is fitting in that he made a living by stones, was killed by their weight and is associated with them after death. The ghost of John Stone also serves as a community memory of the marginalized and often nameless people who worked in the coalfields of southwestern Pennsylvania, ensuring that they will not be forgotten.

Real "Conspiracies": Organizing Labor Unions

While most Irishmen bitterly opposed the union between England and Ireland, there was one kind of union they found necessary. It would be misleading to present Pittsburgh's labor struggles as a solely Irish affair, but the Irish did play key (and sometimes conflicting) roles in the long struggle for the right to collective bargaining and the recognition of labor unions. In legal parlance, union organizing was held to be a conspiracy to fix prices and an infringement on the property rights of the owners of mines, mills and factories. Framing the debate in these terms, capitalists found no shortage of legislators, judges, sheriffs and hired thugs to enforce their interests. Western Pennsylvania's Coal and Iron Police was essentially a private standing army whose purpose was to keep order—as defined by property owners. Drives, strikes and other labor actions were public activities that had to be planned in secret, while the mill and mine owners maintained a network of spies and informers. The Irish often found common cause with Eastern European immigrants who had their own experience with revolutionary struggles and were prepared to fight. This cooperation between immigrant groups was a key component to another violent chapter in the story of the Irish in Pittsburgh: the "Battle of Homestead."

The well-known incident at Andrew Carnegie's Homestead works was precipitated when Carnegie's manager, Henry Clay Frick, attempted to shut out members of the Amalgamated Association of Iron and Steel Workers from the mill and replace them with a new, compliant and presumably more desperate workforce. These replacement workers brought in by mill and mine owners were derisively called "scabs" because they were like the pus-filled covering of a wound. One of the immediate causes for the strike was that Carnegie pulled shenanigans when negotiating wages. Tariffs on imports had historically protected the American steel industry and, consequently, American jobs; thus, it was agreed that wages for all work in the mill would be tied to the tariff-protected "market price" of a single product, the four-inch billet (a small unfinished bar). Carnegie then simply lobbied Congress to change the law, raising the tariff on all other steel products, lowering the tariff on the four-inch billet and thereby crushing wages without breaking the letter of his agreement with his workers. This was a diabolical new wrinkle, and Frick's new sliding wage scale, presented as an ultimatum, would immediately reduce steelworkers' pay by over 20 percent. Plans were made to avert a lockout and deny strikebreakers access to the plant, now dubbed "Fort Frick," as it was hastily fortified with three miles of wooden fence, barbed wire and searchlight towers. When Frick hired a private army of three hundred Pinkerton guards to secure the passage of strikebreakers to Carnegie's property, lookouts were posted along the river to alert Homestead of any approaching mercenaries or strikebreakers. Frick's plan was that the Pinkertons would land on mill property from the river in order to bypass the streets and people of Homestead.

John McLuckie, a steelworker, was the burgess (mayor) of Homestead during the steel lockout and battle. He was the workers' spokesman during the strike, along with union leader Hugh O'Donnell (a name for lost causes, apparently, for three hundred years prior his namesake had joined Hugh O'Neill in the ultimately futile Nine Years' War against the British in Ireland). On June 19, 1892, McLuckie addressed a throng of union men in a speech at the opera house, saying, "We were persuaded to vote the Republican ticket four years ago in order that our wages might be maintained...You men who voted for the Republican ticket voted for high tariff and you get high fences, Pinkerton Detectives, thugs and militia!" The Workers' Advisory Committee at Homestead included quite a few Irishmen: David Shannon, David Lynch, John Coyle, Jack Clifford, William McConeghy, John Durkin, Patrick Fagan, Reid Kennedy, John Murray and Martin Murray. When it was apparent that they would be blamed for any trouble in the upcoming confrontation, they moved to dissolve the committee behind closed doors and then informed the waiting sheriff of their action. This precautionary (and, in actuality, temporary) measure of abdicating responsibility availed them not in the aftermath.

When the approaching three hundred armed Pinkertons were spotted by lookouts, the plant's whistle was sounded at 2:30 a.m. on July 6. The entire community of Homestead sprang into action. A daylong gun battle ensued between two barges full of Pinkertons and workers positioned in and around the pump house. Reporters watched the proceedings in relative safety from the roof of what is now the Bost building and telegraphed the news from the first floor. The Pinkertons were well equipped with repeating rifles, but the workers compensated for the initial disparity in firepower and accuracy by emptying the local ammunition store, deploying a Civil War cannon, lobbing dynamite, improvising incendiary devices and tossing in leftover Independence Day fireworks for good measure. The Pinkertons cowered below decks, unable to get water in the summer heat despite being on the Monongahela River. O'Donnell led the union's Advisory Committee when it imposed a ceasefire and accepted the surrender of the Pinkertons, who were hopelessly pinned down on their barges, with their tugboat driven away by the same heavy fire.

Remarkably, only three Pinkerton agents died in the shootout, and no one was killed in the "running of the gauntlet" that followed the Pinkertons' surrender, when they were beaten and abused by an irate mob. Seven workers died and dozens were injured; most of this grief, however, fell on Pittsburgh's Eastern European communities. The Pennsylvania State Militia occupied the town with a force of 8,500 troops, and the strikers were easily driven from the plant. State authorities immediately reneged on their promise to try the Pinkertons for murder. After the militia occupation, O'Donnell advocated a quick settlement on almost any terms, but the union committee rejected his advice and sacked him. The strike was broken, and O'Donnell left for Mexico, although he later returned to Pittsburgh as a reporter. Meanwhile, the ill-timed shooting of Frick by an anarchist, Alexander Berkman, generated sympathy in the mind of the wider public for the rights of property owners, as did the beating of the

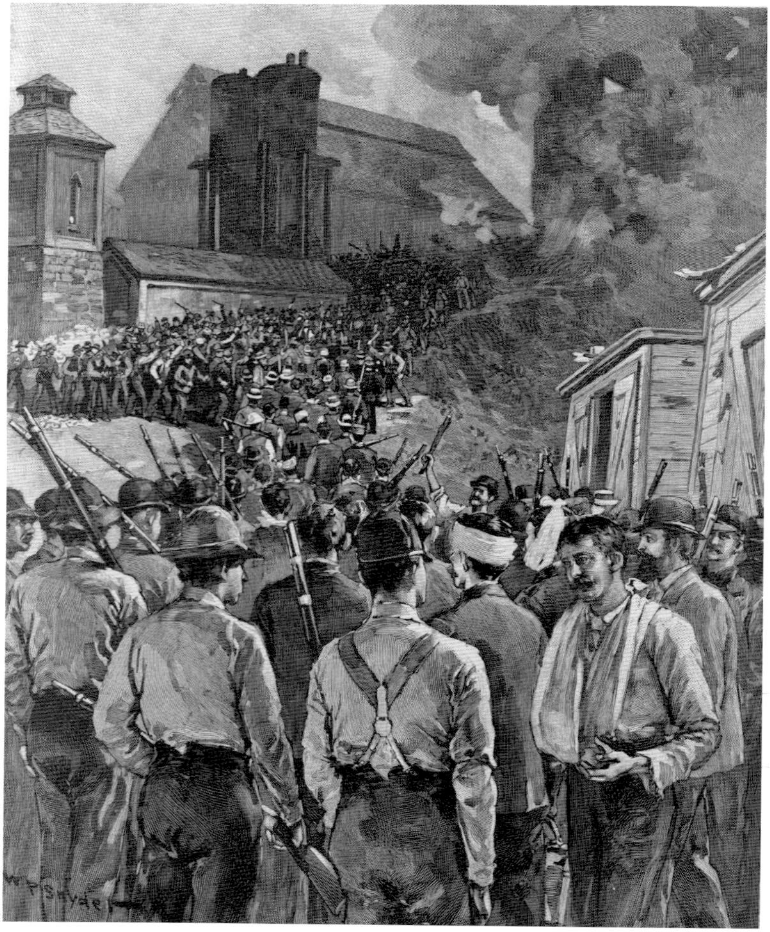

The Homestead riot as drawn by W.P. Snyder for *Harper's Magazine*, July 16, 1892. *Courtesy of the Library of Congress.*

Pinkertons after their surrender. Steelworkers won the Battle of Homestead at Carnegie's steel mill but lost the war, a defeat that crushed unionism in the steel industry for forty-five years. The Amalgamated Association of Iron and Steelworkers rapidly declined from its pre-strike position as the country's most powerful craft union. Many Irish moved into local politics as pro-labor Democrats; however, Republicans were much stronger in Pittsburgh until the 1930s, so an Irish political presence was felt in that party as well. Others, like William Z. Foster, decried the limitations of the American political system and openly advocated Communism.

Part V

TWENTIETH-CENTURY REBELS N'AT, 1914–1945

While some Irish followed the conventions of mainstream participatory democracy, working with the Democratic or Republican Parties, others felt that the existing power structure merely facilitated the suppression of workers' rights. Irish Pittsburghers became some of the leading radicals of the day. Some of them, such as Fannie Sellins, John Fitzpatrick and William Z. Foster, became major figures in the great 1919 steel strike and beyond, despite the fact that none of them had ever worked in steel.

Following the 1919 strike, steel unions were crushed. However, when unions achieved legitimacy and legal protection as part of Franklin Delano Roosevelt's New Deal during the Depression, Irish leaders again played an important role. No one was more influential than Phillip Murray. Born in Scotland but of Irish Donegal roots, the sixteen-year-old Murray came to the United States in 1902. Already a coal miner and union member when he arrived in western Pennsylvania, he rapidly advanced in the leadership of the United Mine Workers of America. At the age of thirty-two, in 1915, he became president of District Five, representing workers in the heart of western Pennsylvania's coalfields. His experience during World War I on the National Bituminous Coal Production Committee and Pennsylvania Regional War Labor Board led him to take an accommodating or even conservative approach to labor-management relations. He viewed labor-government-business boards and government intervention in general as being useful to the interests of labor.

Murray became a trusted lieutenant of John L. Lewis, president of the United Mine Workers of America. John Lewis promoted industrial unionism as president of the Congress of Industrial Organizations (CIO), and he chose Phillip Murray to head the Steel Workers Organizing Committee (SWOC) in 1936. The SWOC had spectacular success in capturing the company unions that U.S. Steel had formed. Another Irish leader in this effort was Elmer Maloy, who headed the company union at the corporation's Duquesne works and was elected mayor of Duquesne in 1937. The SWOC, riding the momentum of Roosevelt's 1936 presidential victory, managed to get the company unions to adopt SWOC's wage and hour demands. On July 5, 1936, organizers under Pat Fagan and Emmet Patrick Cush, the sons of 1892 strikers, opened the CIO organizing drive in steel with a meeting at the graves of the 1892 union dead. As the company union representatives turned to the CIO, the rank and file followed. This organizing momentum inside the steel corporation's plants, however, was considerably slowed by the unexpectedly negotiated union recognition agreement devised by Lewis and U.S. Steel's Myron Taylor. Phillip Murray succeeded Lewis as president of the CIO, became the first president of the United Steelworkers of America and served on an "alphabet soup" of government boards during World War II.

Martyrs

For slavery fled O glorious dead when you fell in the foggy dew.
—*Canon Charles O'Neill*

In 1916, Irishmen again rebelled against British domination and proclaimed a republic that was quelled within a few days by British troops and artillery. Most of the leaders who proclaimed the new republic from the Dublin Courthouse were executed, including Patrick Pearse, Thomas MacDonagh, Thomas Clarke and Joseph Plunkett. The ill-coordinated uprising failed to gain widespread support, but the subsequent British occupation of Dublin and mass incarceration of suspects decisively shifted public opinion in favor of republicanism. The Irish events of 1916 were not unnoticed in Pittsburgh; for years afterward, requiem masses, memorial banquets and speeches were given in their honor throughout Pittsburgh. Today, while many drunken revelers may not be paying attention to the lyrics, songs like "Foggy Dew" remain St. Patrick's Day staples for local bands. Likewise, Fannie (Mooney) Sellins served as Pittsburgh's labor martyr in the era immediately following

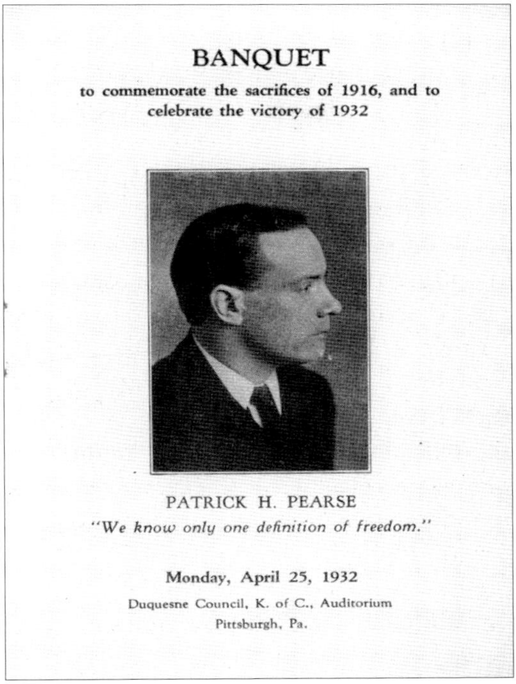

BANQUET

to commemorate the sacrifices of 1916, and to celebrate the victory of 1932

PATRICK H. PEARSE

"We know only one definition of freedom."

Monday, April 25, 1932

Duquesne Council, K. of C., Auditorium

Pittsburgh, Pa.

Right: Irish Independence Club banquet program for April 25, 1932. *Courtesy of Archives Service Center, University of Pittsburgh.*

Below: Martyrs of 1916 Mass card, April 18, 1920. *Courtesy of Archives Service Center, University of Pittsburgh.*

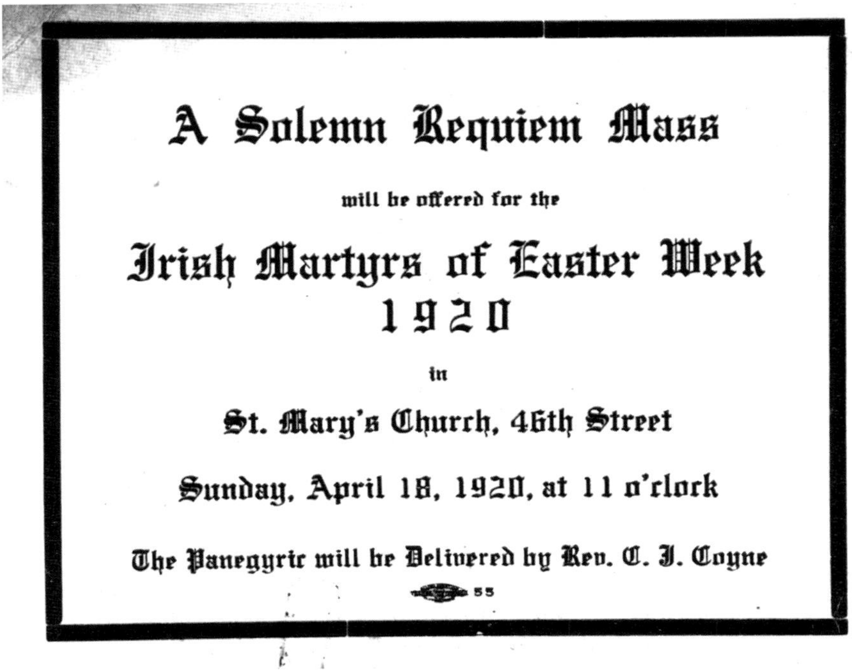

A Solemn Requiem Mass

will be offered for the

Irish Martyrs of Easter Week

1920

in

St. Mary's Church, 46th Street

Sunday, April 18, 1920, at 11 o'clock

The Panegyric will be Delivered by Rev. C. J. Coyne

55

The Irish Martyrs of 1916

PATRICK H. PEARSE
THOMAS MacDONAGH
MICHAEL O'HANRAHAN
EDWARD DALY
CORNELIUS COLBERT
MICHAEL MALLON
JAMES CONNOLLY
THOMAS J. CLARKE
JOSEPH PLUNKETT
MAJ. JOHN MacBRIDE
WILLIAM PEARSE
EDMUND KENT
J. J. HEUSTON
JOHN McDERMOTT
THOMAS KENT
F. SHEEHY SKEFFINGTON
ROGER CASEMENT

Memorial Mass Meeting

Friends of Irish Freedom
LYCEUM THEATRE
PITTSBURGH
April 11th, 1920

A flyer for a martyrs of 1916 public meeting at Lyceum Theater, April 11, 1920. *Courtesy of Archives Service Center, University of Pittsburgh.*

World War I and is today commemorated in a ballad by Irish contemporary Pittsburgh activist Ann Feeney:

> *In the company slums of Ducktown in the summer of nineteen,*
> *An unarmed striking miner was gunned down by deputies.*
> *When Fannie cried out, "Spare his life!" They shot her down as well.*
> *And hundreds watched in horror as this fearless woman fell.*

Yet another violent chapter in Pittsburgh's history began as the end of World War I led to a decline in demand for steel and companies began to squeeze workers to maintain profits. It was obvious to all that another major steel strike was forthcoming. The 1919 steel strike mobilized workers against an industry that featured brutal twelve-hour days in unsafe working conditions for six or seven days a week. An unskilled and semi-skilled workforce that was mostly composed of Eastern Europeans was led by prominent strike leaders and radicals of Irish descent, including William Z. Foster, John Fitzpatrick, Mary Harris "Mother" Jones and Fannie Sellins. None of them had ever worked in the steel industry, but they successfully transferred the skills of labor organizing gained during their earlier employment in other industries. For instance, Fannie (Mooney) Sellins had moved to Pittsburgh from St. Louis, where she had worked in the garment industry and became a union leader fighting for about four hundred seamstresses in a successful strike that lasted twenty-five months. A widowed mother of four children, she was one of the few female leaders of the United Garment Workers of America (UGWA) in 1910. In 1913, she came to Pittsburgh for the UGWA. After visiting the coalfields, however, she began doing relief work and then organizing for the United Mine Workers of America (UMWA) in Collier, West Virginia, just across the state line. After defying a court injunction, she was jailed for three months until pardoned by President Woodrow Wilson in 1916. A court order had prohibited all union organizing, and she vehemently spoke against judicial attempts to suppress her First Amendment rights to freedom of speech and assembly: "I am free and I have the right to walk or talk any place in this country, as long as I obey the law. The only wrong they can say I've done is to take shoes to the little children in Collier who needed shoes."

Upon her return to Pittsburgh, Sellins was hired to the staff of UMWA District Five by Phil Murray. As strikes loomed in 1917, many of the strikebreaking scabs were African Americans from the South who were frequently offered employment under false pretenses and were unaware that they were being shipped north to cross picket lines and break strikes. On February 24, 1917, Sellins met a trainload of these strikebreakers at the Tarentum station and persuaded many of them to join the workers in New Kensington instead. In the summer of 1919, she was again sent to the Allegheny-Kiskiminetas Valley region to direct picketing miners in the employ of Allegheny Coke and Coal, an Allegheny Steel subsidiary. The mostly Polish workers in the company town of West Natrona raised ducks for food, hence the "Ducktown" moniker. This time the scabs were Greeks and "free-born Americans." Several black miners were present with Sellins on the day she was killed, a testimony to both Sellins's earlier persuasive efforts and the workers' more inclusive definition of "union."

Accounts of her death at the hands of sheriff's deputies on August 26, 1919, are wildly inconsistent, but it is safe to say that there were two narratives: one told by and for labor and one told by the steel industry to legitimize its actions before the wider American public. In one narrative, Sellins was protecting children and denouncing the deputized goons who had just fatally shot a worker, Joseph Starzelski. In the industry version, she was a dangerous criminal among a group of workers who had opened fire with pistols from the nearby Ducktown hilltop. What is indisputable is that Sellins was brutally beaten and shot (not necessarily in that order) near the gates of Allegheny Steel in Brackenridge, Pennsylvania.

Consequently, her caved-in face appeared on a flyer with the headline "Shall Fiendish Cruelty Rule America." This sad picture was to be found in nearly every union hall or office during the 1919 steel strike. Despite numerous eyewitnesses, the Allegheny coroner's jury attributed her death to "person or persons unknown" during an attack on sheriff's deputies. The jurors were successfully convinced that a riot had occurred; therefore, everyone present was guilty of rioting. The jury's findings reflected the rhetoric of the postwar red scare when it added, "We also criticize and deplore the actions of Alien or Agitators who instill Anarchy and Bolshevism Doctrines in the minds of UnAmericans [*sic*] and uneducated Aliens."

Sheriff Haddock later complained to a Senate labor committee that Sellins's body had been dug up and mutilated in a ghoulish propaganda scheme. The August 12, 1920 edition of the *Iron Age* resorted to similar preposterous claims in order to uphold the steel industry; George Smart insisted that the purported photo of Sellins could have been anybody and maintained that a photograph of Pennsylvania's mounted police terrorizing local residents and shopkeepers in Clairton had been staged with the complicity of labor-friendly officers, saying of the union organizers, "In their dire distress, these enterprising artists appealed to members of the constabulary, who although frequently charged with brutality, demonstrated their good nature by consenting to the request to pose for pictures showing how violence would be carried on if there should be any." William Z. Foster later attacked these claims in *The Freeman*, and his credible defense of the provenance of the Clairton picture noted that it had run in the *New York Times* before coming to the attention of the strike committee. Ultimately, disputing the provenance of "Fannie Sellins" images, whether on flyers in 1919 or on the Internet today, is simply a distraction from the events surrounding her death.

When the big strike came, it was at first successful in Gary and Johnstown but was ultimately broken in Pittsburgh's Monongahela Valley, where Slavic workers went for solidarity but most English-speaking second- and third-generation workers stayed on the job. Furthermore, the boll weevil infestation was devastating cotton growers in the South and prompting the start of the first "Great Migration," which provided an increasing flow of black workers who could be used as strikebreakers. These internal divisions within the working class made the union no match for the wealth and power of the steel companies and its political allies.

Labor was again defeated in the Steel City, although steelworkers in Allegheny Valley mill towns such as Natrona and Brackenridge walked off their jobs. The steel company maintained that Starzelski was a strikebreaker shot by disorderly labor agitators, not a union man shot by sheriff's deputies, so they could say that one of their own had been killed. This claim is doubtful, however; Joseph Starzelski was memorialized along with Fannie Sellins on the UMWA monument in the Union Cemetery outside New Kensington. Fannie Sellins has largely faded into obscurity outside of labor circles, but the Irish martyrs of 1916 are commemorated at the Dublin Post Office, at the burial yard in old Arbor Hill prison, in countless murals across Ireland and in Pittsburgh's Irish culture.

De Valera Visits Pittsburgh

The postwar era was a momentous one for the Irish community, both worldwide and in Pittsburgh. England, exhausted from years of trench warfare against Germany in World War I, finally lost its grip on Ireland after a successful war of independence was fought from 1919 to 1921. This was followed by a civil war lasting until May 1923, a set of events far beyond the scope of this book. It must suffice to note that twenty-six of Ireland's thirty-two counties were finally breaking free of English rule; however, official American political support in the form of diplomatic recognition was not forthcoming. Eamon de Valera, a survivor of the failed 1916 Easter Week rising in Dublin, now represented the Irish Republic. He had famously escaped from Lincoln Prison in England and was a wanted fugitive there. Entering the United States as a stowaway without a passport, he championed the fledgling Irish government and its fighters, who were in dire need of both political legitimacy and money. Consequently, as the president of the Irish Republic, de Valera spent eighteen months seeking recognition of his government and persuading the scattered sons and daughters of Erin to buy bonds and support the fight in Ireland. Pittsburgh rose to the occasion on October 4, 1919.

An estimated ten thousand people gathered to hear and meet de Valera at a public reception hosted by the Associated Irish-American Societies of Western Pennsylvania at the Syria Mosque. Anticipating an overflow crowd, Soldiers and Sailors Memorial Hall was booked for a second engagement, and each speaker hurried from the Syria Mosque to repeat his address at Memorial Hall. The *Pittsburgh Press* had published a veritable "Who's Who in Irish Pittsburgh" the day before, listing dozens of prominent Pittsburghers and social organizations, including the Ancient Order of Hibernians and its Women's Auxiliary, Catholic Women's League, Clan na Gael, Friends of Irish Freedom, Knights of Equity, Irish Catholic Benevolent Union and the Irish Freedom Fund. Due to a misunderstanding, however, de Valera did not receive an honorary degree from Duquesne University, as originally planned.

De Valera appealed to his Pittsburgh audience for American recognition of the sovereignty of the Irish Republic, but according to the *Gazette Times*, "Irish enthusiasm could not be contained...he was frequently interrupted by handclapping and applause." The words of Harry Boland, secretary of Sinn Fein and member of the National Congress of Ireland, were recorded for posterity. Pointing to Woodrow Wilson's principle of self-determination and reviewing Ireland's long struggle under England's domination, Boland said, "America can, by setting the proper example in this clear case of Ireland, make the principle of self-determination a recognized principle of international law—and really make the world safe for democracy." Boland cited the recent election results, where 80 percent of the people sought an end to the union with England. He also lamented the seventy-year decline in Irish population from eight million to only four million and asked Pittsburghers "not to encourage anyone to leave the land, but on the contrary, to send back as many as you can." Rather than encourage young Irishmen to leave, Americans were exhorted to send men and money to the fight at home. De Valera and his party sold 300,000 bonds, raising $5 million on their epic tour. The back-to-back rallies in Pittsburgh were part of what has been described as "the greatest speaking tour ever."

Not everyone in Pittsburgh was cheering, though. At that very moment, the Pennsylvania branch of the American Legion was voicing its objections to support of de Valera's new government, claiming that de Valera and his party had handicapped Great Britain and the Allies in World War I. This dissenting voice of the American Legion, claiming Irish disloyalty, grew louder as de Valera's tour progressed westward across America. The resolution of the Pennsylvania American Legion was subsequently entered into the congressional record by James S. McGraw, a Presbyterian minister from Pittsburgh. Lord Beaverbrook, the British newspaper mogul and former minister of information during World War I, had advocated in his *Sunday Express* column the use of American Methodists and Presbyterians to "crush the Sinn Feiners as a cartwheel crushes a toad." McGraw's testimony and the influence of the American Legion were important spokes in the looming cartwheel.

This campaign of orchestrating opposition to American recognition of an Irish nation was successful. In November 1919, a congressional committee was considering the Mason Bill, which would have allocated $14,000 to cover the salaries of diplomats for relations with the new Irish Republic. At issue was not the money but the possibility of provoking England by recognizing the sovereignty of an Irish rebel government at war with England and the question of whether America was willing to fight for Irish self-determination, if necessary. The tensions with England were palpable, although the newspaper of Ireland's Sinn Fein Party was prone to exaggerate them. The ferocious hearings in Congress led nowhere; the Mason Bill died in committee in 1920, and the Irish had to wait until 1924 for American recognition of the Irish Free State. The cost of peace in the Anglo-Irish treaty of 1921 was the permanent division of Ireland and other onerous terms imposed by the English. As the pro-treaty side won the Irish civil war, de Valera and other Irish Republican Army irregulars were hunted down by the new Irish Free State. After a brief imprisonment, de Valera reluctantly took a loyalty oath as he planned a new republican party, Fianna Fail, and a metropolitan daily paper that would serve as the party organ.

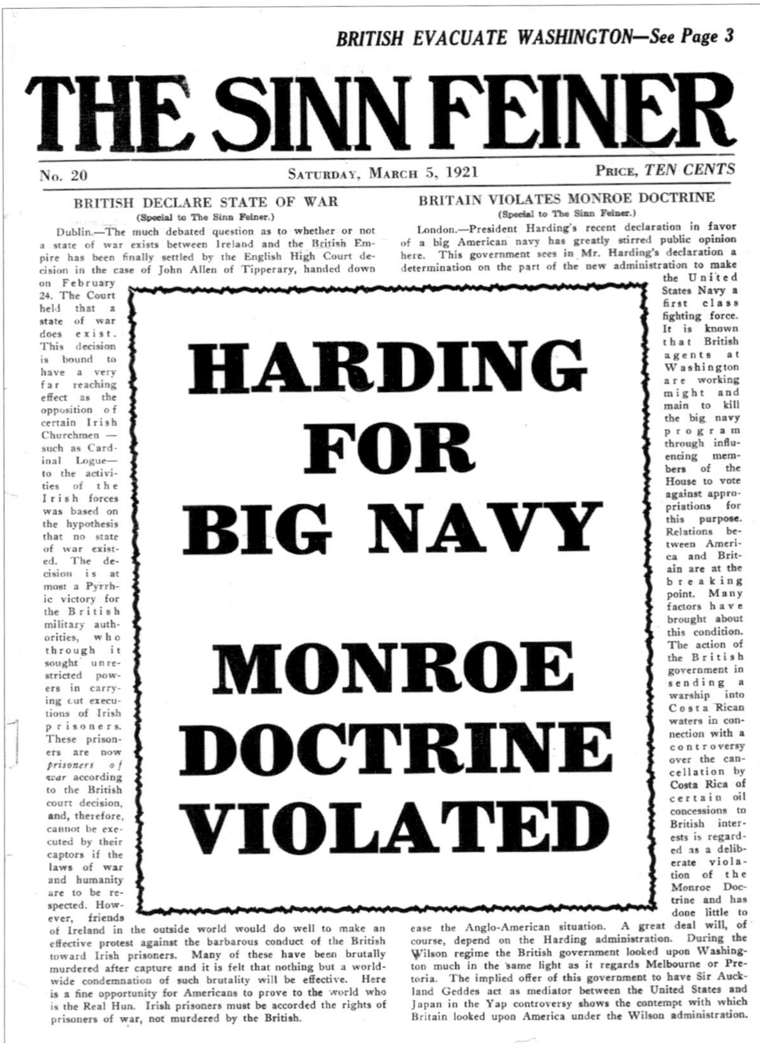

BRITISH EVACUATE WASHINGTON—See Page 3

THE SINN FEINER

No. 20 | SATURDAY, MARCH 5, 1921 | PRICE, *TEN CENTS*

BRITISH DECLARE STATE OF WAR

(Special to The Sinn Feiner.)

Dublin.—The much debated question as to whether or not a state of war exists between Ireland and the British Empire has been finally settled by the English High Court decision in the case of John Allen of Tipperary, handed down on February 24. The Court held that a state of war does exist. This decision is bound to have a very far reaching effect as the opposition of certain Irish Churchmen — such as Cardinal Logue— to the activities of the Irish forces was based on the hypothesis that no state of war existed. The decision is at most a Pyrrhic victory for the British military authorities, who through it sought unrestricted powers in carrying out executions of Irish prisoners. These prisoners are now *prisoners of war* according to the British court decision, and, therefore, cannot be executed by their captors if the laws of war and humanity are to be respected. However, friends of Ireland in the outside world would do well to make an effective protest against the barbarous conduct of the British toward Irish prisoners. Many of these have been brutally murdered after capture and it is felt that nothing but a world-wide condemnation of such brutality will be effective. Here is a fine opportunity for Americans to prove to the world who is the Real Hun. Irish prisoners must be accorded the rights of prisoners of war, not murdered by the British.

HARDING FOR BIG NAVY

MONROE DOCTRINE VIOLATED

BRITAIN VIOLATES MONROE DOCTRINE

(Special to The Sinn Feiner.)

London.—President Harding's recent declaration in favor of a big American navy has greatly stirred public opinion here. This government sees in Mr. Harding's declaration a determination on the part of the new administration to make the United States Navy a first class fighting force. It is known that British agents at Washington are working might and main to kill the big navy program through influencing members of the House to vote against appropriations for this purpose. Relations between America and Britain are at the breaking point. Many factors have brought about this condition. The action of the British government in sending a warship into Costa Rican waters in connection with a controversy over the cancellation by Costa Rica of certain oil concessions to British interests is regarded as a deliberate violation of the Monroe Doctrine and has done little to ease the Anglo-American situation. A great deal will, of course, depend on the Harding administration. During the Wilson regime the British government looked upon Washington much in the same light as it regards Melbourne or Pretoria. The implied offer of this government to have Sir Auckland Geddes act as mediator between the United States and Japan in the Yap controversy shows the contempt with which Britain looked upon America under the Wilson administration.

Sinn Feiner, March 5, 1921. *Courtesy of Archives Service Center, University of Pittsburgh.*

De Valera returned to Pittsburgh in 1930 as former president of the Irish Republic, seeking support for the Irish Press, Ltd., of Dublin. Founded in 1928, the paper was still struggling to launch, and de Valera had a fundraising plan to present to Pittsburgh's Irish community. John B. Collins, an active member of the Pittsburgh chapter of the American Association for the Recognition of the Irish Republic (AARIR) and the Friends of

Irish Freedom (FOIF) during the 1920s and '30s, was among those instrumental in arranging de Valera's visit. Pittsburghers who purchased Irish government bonds could now assign the interest payments to the Irish Press, supporting both the new country and a proposed voice for the Irish people. Speaking again at Soldiers and Sailors Memorial on March 25, 1930, de Valera promised his audience "a newspaper that will be free from entangling alliances. Its columns will be open to the people and we will print all the news in an unbiased way." He also strongly objected to the $26 million a year Ireland was compelled to pay to England, saying, "Lloyd George told me that if the treaty were not accepted Ireland would be crushed in war." The Irish Free State had been forced to assume responsibility for a proportionate part of the United Kingdom's debt and was therefore bankrolling England's war debts. In addition to speechmaking, de Valera met with

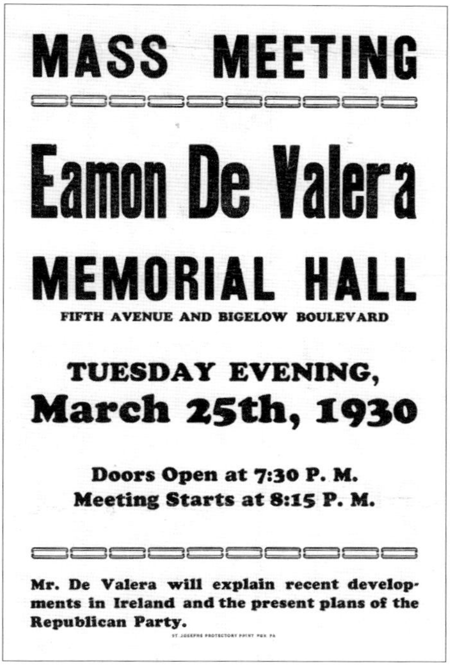

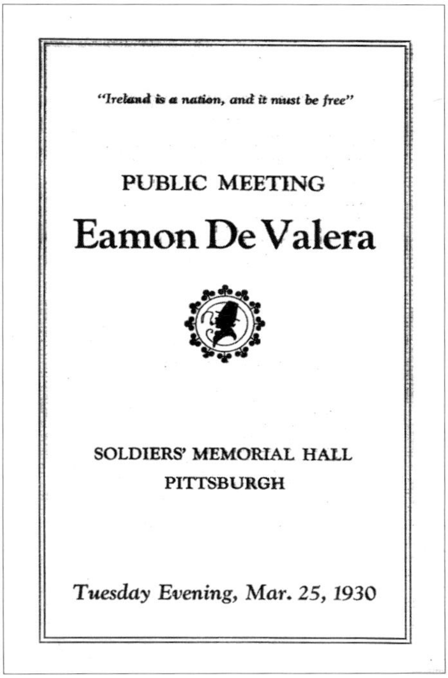

This page: Fliers promoting de Valera's Pittsburgh appearance on March 25, 1930. *Courtesy of Archives Service Center, University of Pittsburgh.*

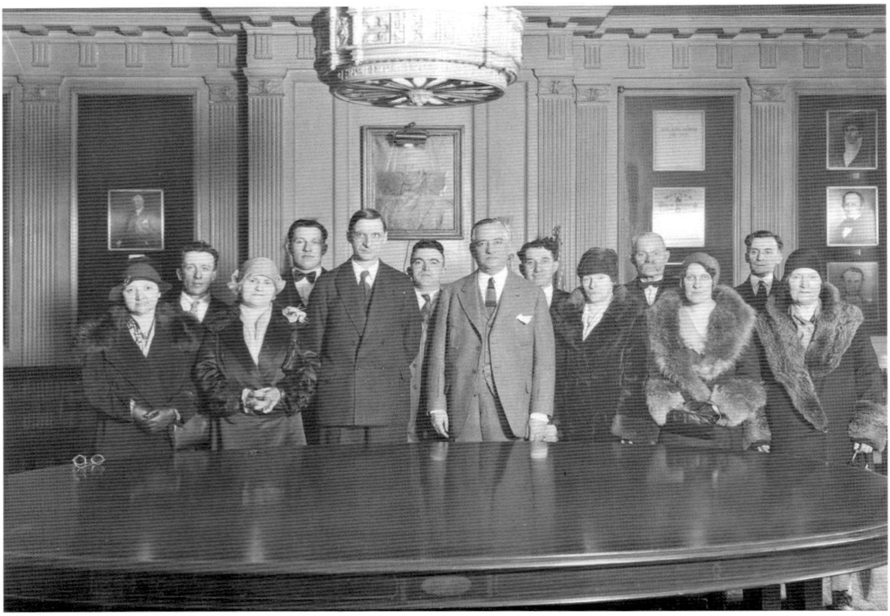

De Valera (fifth from left) with Mayor Charles H. Kline (seventh from right) and others, March 1930. *Courtesy of Archives Service Center, University of Pittsburgh.*

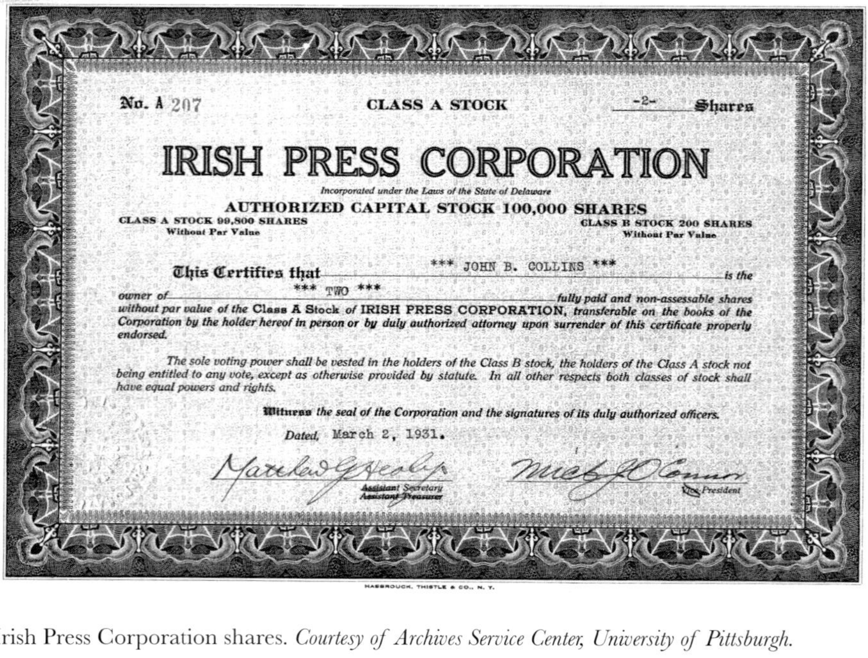

No. A 207 CLASS A STOCK -2- Shares

IRISH PRESS CORPORATION

Incorporated under the Laws of the State of Delaware

AUTHORIZED CAPITAL STOCK 100,000 SHARES

CLASS A STOCK 99,800 SHARES Without Par Value

CLASS B STOCK 200 SHARES Without Par Value

This Certifies that *** JOHN B. COLLINS *** *is the owner of* *** TWO *** *fully paid and non-assessable shares without par value of the* **Class A Stock** *of* **IRISH PRESS CORPORATION**, *transferable on the books of the Corporation by the holder hereof in person or by duly authorized attorney upon surrender of this certificate properly endorsed.*

The sole voting power shall be vested in the holders of the Class B stock, the holders of the Class A stock not being entitled to any vote, except as otherwise provided by statute. In all other respects both classes of stock shall have equal powers and rights.

Witness *the seal of the Corporation and the signatures of its duly authorized officers.*

Dated, March 2, 1931.

Assistant Secretary ~~*Assistant Treasurer*~~

Vice President

HASBROUCK, THISTLE & CO., N. Y.

Irish Press Corporation shares. *Courtesy of Archives Service Center, University of Pittsburgh.*

local Irish leaders and Mayor Charles Howard Kline. De Valera also took the time to visit the Pittsburgh press, intending to gain practical information on the running of a metropolitan daily newspaper. De Valera and his new party were successful for many years to come, thanks to contributions from prominent Irish Pittsburghers such as John Collins.

The Klan Provokes the Ire of Carnegie, Pennsylvania

The 1920s saw a resurgence of bigotry in America. The movie *Birth of a Nation* promoted white supremacy and glorified the Ku Klux Klan, stirring up long-smoldering resentments, and western Pennsylvania became a Klan stronghold. Public rallies were held, at which thousands of new members were initiated. One such recruitment effort in Carnegie, Pennsylvania, ended disastrously in 1923. The Klan selected Carnegie for a massive August 25 gathering because the town's population of 2,500 was evenly split between Protestants and Catholics. A perceived failure to enforce Prohibition (which always had anti-immigrant and anti-Irish undertones) by local officials in Carnegie and nearby McKees Rocks was a local grievance. The planned event was bound to provoke a sizable counter-rally, and trouble was all but guaranteed. Yes, dear readers, it's time for still another violent chapter in the saga of Irish Pittsburgh.

Between ten and twenty-five thousand people from Pennsylvania and nearby states assembled at a twenty-acre site on Forsythe's hill. The day's events featured songs, fireworks and speeches encouraging visitors to join the Klan for a fifteen-dollar fee. The self-proclaimed "invisible empire" of the Klan gained one thousand members early that evening. At 8:30 p.m., the national leader of the Klan, Imperial Wizard Wesley Hiram Evans, arrived to lead the parade through Carnegie. Fearing violence, Carnegie deputy sheriffs informed the Klansmen that their permit to march was denied. The Klansmen interpreted this message from Mayor John F. Conley as a Catholic challenge, and at 10:30 p.m., five thousand Klansmen and recent inductees marched downhill toward Carnegie.

At the edge of town, they found that the Pan Handle Railway Bridge had been obstructed by trucks, so they changed their route and headed to the Glendale Bridge, which was only lightly blocked by a single car. Carnegie residents rushed to the Glendale Bridge as well. The Klan wanted more than a parade, as they deliberately attempted a route that would take them

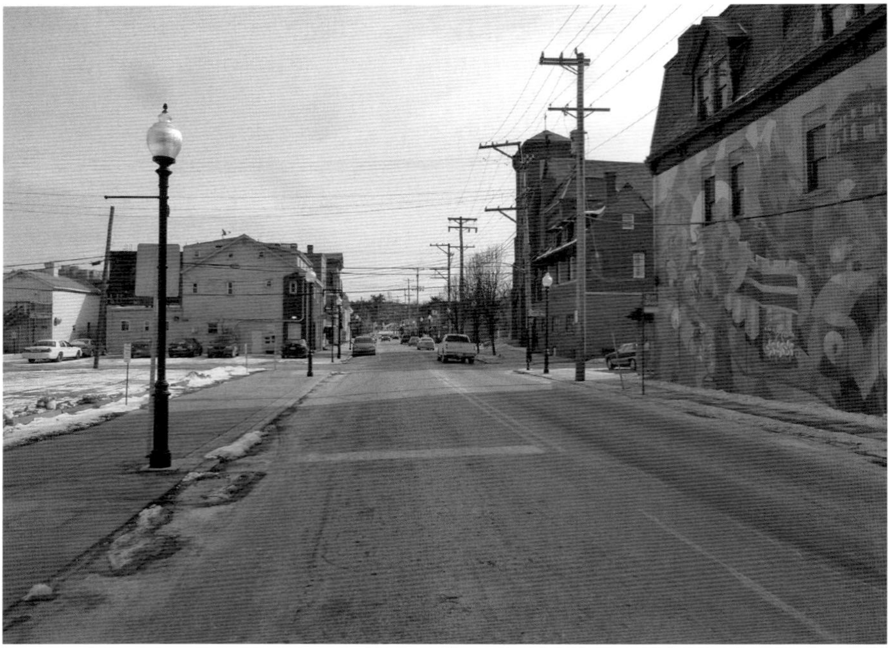

Where the Klan was stopped at Third Avenue and Barrett Street, Carnegie, Pennsylvania. *Courtesy of Janis Ferrainolo.*

before Catholic churches. It was nearing midnight as the Klan procession made its way through the section of Carnegie known as Irishtown, and the police were unable to restrain a one-thousand-strong hostile mob that assaulted the marchers in a chaotic mêlée of clubs, rocks and bricks. "Hoods were knocked off; robes torn," according to the *Pittsburgh Post*, and nearby rail cars provided a limitless source for the lumps of coal that served as "Irish confetti." Shooting began as the front of the parade reached St. Luke's Catholic Church at Barrett Way and Third Street. Thomas Abbott, a newly inducted Klan member, was shot in the head across the street from the church and died shortly afterward. Some Klansmen removed their robes and hoods, attempting to flee, while others carried away wounded comrades. When the deputy sheriffs pleaded again for an end to the march, the Klansmen retreated to Forsythe's Farm, leaving the streets of Carnegie covered in blood, weapons and Klan hoods. Neighborhood lore says that the shooters were in the church bell towers.

In the aftermath, the Carnegie police could find no one to testify against the rioters. They did arrest a local undertaker, Patrick McDermott, for the murder of Thomas Abbott, but a lack of evidence led to his acquittal by a coroner's jury. Abbott's widow pushed for a trial, which took place in November 1924. Witness testimony was contradictory and inconclusive. McDermott was a respectable member of the Carnegie community, and the jury took only forty-seven minutes to acquit him.

Despite its ignominious retreat from Carnegie, the riot was a propaganda coup for the Klan; it had both a martyr and an Irish Catholic scapegoat. Although he later denied it, Imperial Wizard Evans reportedly said that night that Abbott's death was worth twenty-five thousand new members for the Klan. The language in the Klan's subsequent tribute to a fallen "warrior for Christ," *The Martyred Klansman*, would have suited the anti-Catholic and anti-immigrant Know-Nothings of the previous century: "The dastardly deeds of an enemy trampling the stars and stripes of this country…unwarranted attempts to injure and maim native-born Americans…Our only aim is that one hundred per cent Protestants may know of the passing of one of their unselfish brothers." Ultimately, greed and internal fighting destroyed the strength and influence of the Klan in western Pennsylvania more than any external factor. Today, Klan activity is generally associated with southern states in the American mind, but the Irish, as usual, have long memories and enjoy claiming that Carnegie, Pennsylvania, was where the Klan was broken.

Father James Renshaw Cox

Have you ever heard someone say "enough food to feed Cox's army"? Father James Renshaw Cox, a pastor of St. Patrick's Church in the Strip District, was known for his pro-labor activism. In early 1930, he organized a massive protest march of unemployed men on Washington, D.C. Born in the Lawrenceville neighborhood of Pittsburgh, he was familiar with the hardships of the working man. A cab driver and steelworker, he worked his way through Duquesne University and entered St. Vincent Seminary in Latrobe before serving as a chaplain in World War I. After the war, he earned a master of economics degree from the University of Pittsburgh.

In 1923, Father James Cox became pastor of the declining St. Patrick's Church, at its third location in Pittsburgh's Strip District. The expansion of business in the area had pushed out many residents, but Father Cox revitalized the parish, and in 1924, it became the "American Shrine to Our

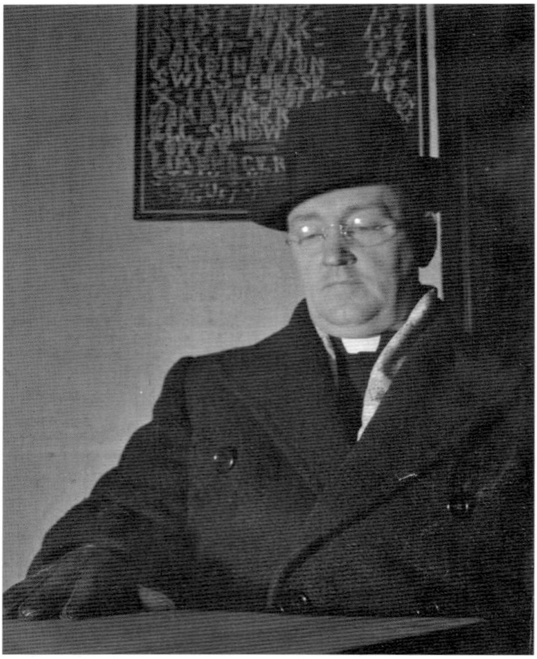

Left: Father James Renshaw Cox. *Courtesy of St. Patrick–St. Stanislaus Kostka Parish Archives.*

Below: The Strip District shantytown near St. Patrick's. *Courtesy of Photo Antiquities.*

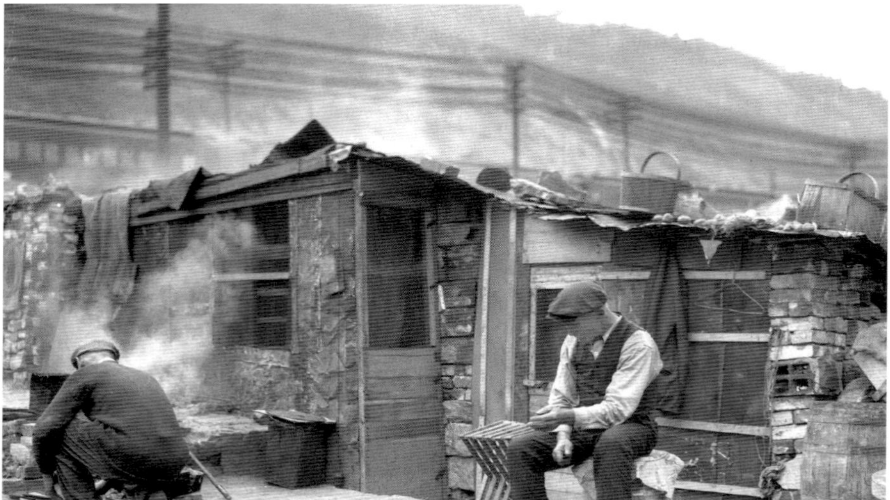

Lady of Lourdes" in thanks for the healing of his eyes at Lourdes earlier. In 1925, Father Cox began broadcasting from St. Patrick's Church on WJAS, a gig that would last for thirty-three years. His social awareness homilies made him a nationally known labor priest and a central figure in Pittsburgh's own "Catholic New Deal." But works were needed more than words, and as the Great Depression spread, a shantytown sprang up alongside the parish in the Strip from 1929 to 1932. Under Father Cox's direction, St. Patrick's became a center of relief for the poor. With the help of underemployed cab drivers, he set up a soup kitchen, collecting food and clothing and distributing over two million free meals and half a million baskets of food, clothing and fuel.

This assistance to the poor was far from adequate; what was needed was unprecedented action at the national level. In what became the largest demonstration to date in the nation's capital, Cox led a march of twenty-five thousand unemployed Pennsylvanians to Washington, D.C. Known as "Cox's Army," they drove their jalopies and trucks over the Allegheny Mountains to present their "Petition of the Unemployed" to the House and Senate. They slept on the roadside and in church basements, jailhouses or any space offered to them. And they sang:

When you are poor, 'tis hard to hear, the babies cry for bread,
And all you have to offer them, is tales of hope instead,
When little feet are cold and bare, on bodies poorly clad,
Kind soothing words are little use, to make that heart feel glad.
I want a job, a steady job; a job with decent pay,
Where I can work and earn enough to keep the wolf away,
To have a roof over my head, a fire to keep warm,
Where I can take a nightly rest, that strength renew my arm.

Father Cox hoped the action would stir Congress and President Herbert Hoover to start a public works program and to raise the inheritance tax to 70 percent. Hoover and the Republican National Committee, embarrassed by the marchers, had them investigated. They suspected that the Vatican or Democratic supporters of Al Smith (the Catholic presidential candidate who had lost to Hoover in 1928) were secretly bankrolling the marchers' gasoline purchases on their way to Washington. It turned out that Andrew Mellon had quietly ordered his Gulf Oil gas stations to give free gas to the marchers, an interesting move from the scion of one of Pittsburgh's founding families whose

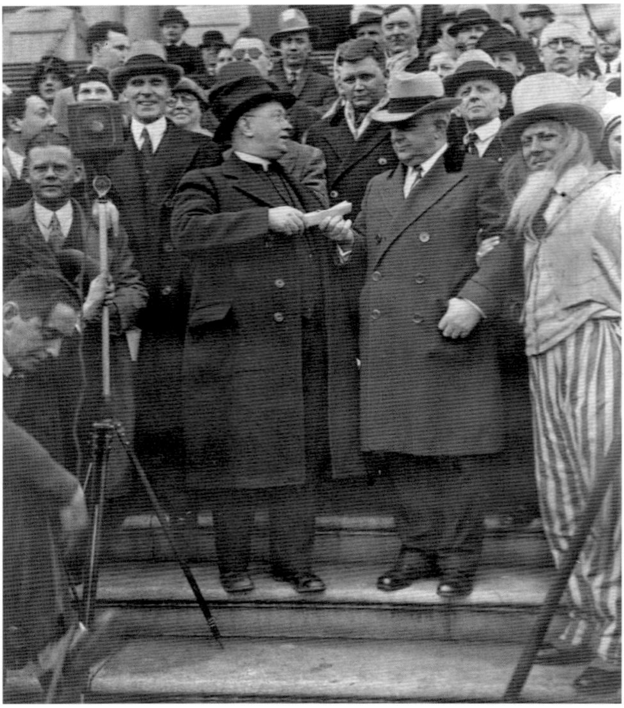

Left: Father Cox presenting the Jobless Petition to Congress. *Courtesy of St. Patrick–St. Stanislaus Kostka Parish Archives.*

Below: Marchers setting forth, January 15, 1930. *Courtesy of St. Patrick–St. Stanislaus Kostka Parish Archives.*

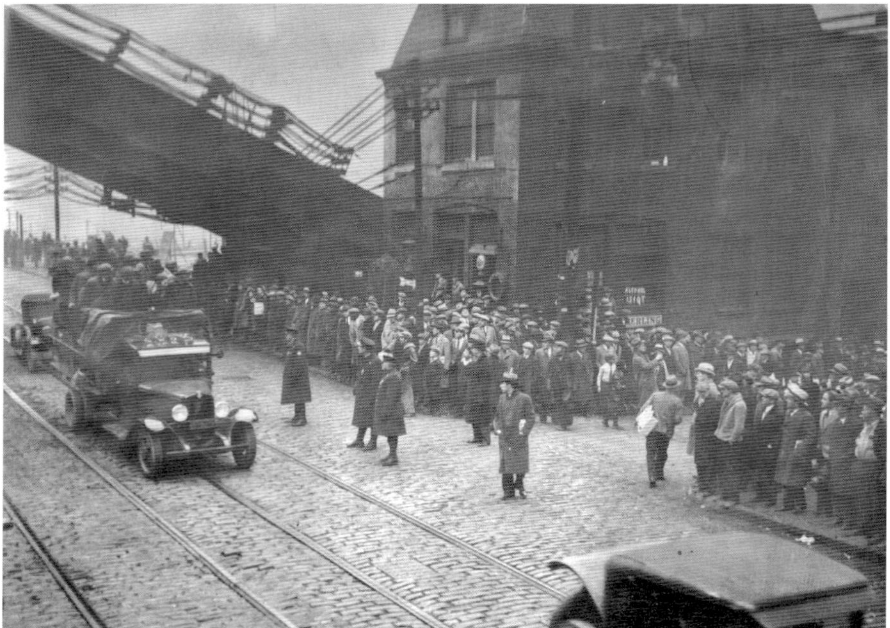

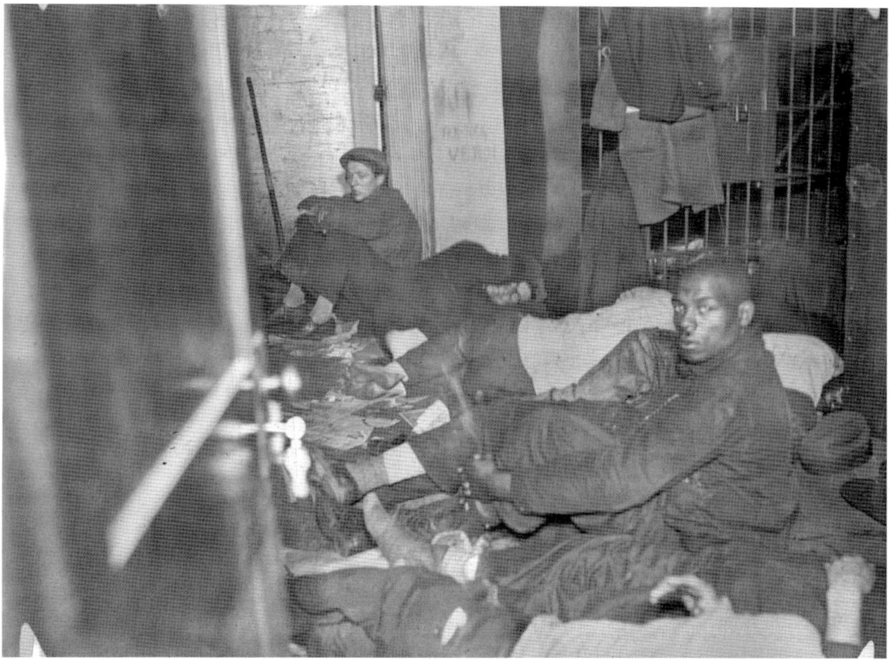

Marchers sleeping in a jailhouse. *Courtesy of St. Patrick–St. Stanislaus Kostka Parish Archives.*

generational wealth transfers would have been hard hit by Cox's proposed inheritance tax. The marchers received a heroes' welcome upon their return, but the federal government was slow to respond to an apparently intractable crisis of capitalism that left an estimated 25 percent of Americans unemployed.

In 1932, Father Cox ran for president of the United States on the Jobless Party ticket, receiving 250,000 votes. Afterward, he continued his relief work as a member of the Pennsylvania Commission for the Unemployed, and in the mid-'30s, President Roosevelt appointed him to the state recovery board of the National Recovery Administration. Known as Pittsburgh's "Pastor of the Poor," Cox was also a mentor to Father Charles Owen Rice, who would inherit his mantle as Pittsburgh's labor priest after Cox's death in 1951.

St. Patrick's Church was destroyed by fire in March 1935, but Bishop Hugh C. Boyle told Father Cox not to build another church. This is why the fourth St. Patrick's Church looks more like a house or chapel than a church and why, surrounded by a Pittsburgh-weathered wall, it can be

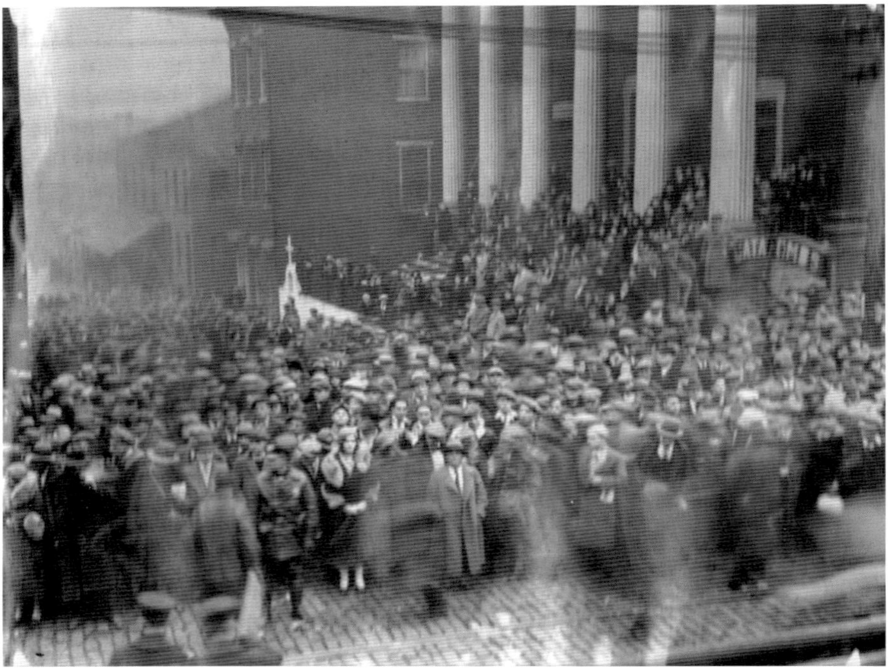

A heroes' welcome at the front of St. Patrick's. *Courtesy of St. Patrick–St. Stanislaus Kostka Parish Archives.*

readily mistaken as an old original church. The catacombs were removed when building the new church. The turrets of the extant church, dedicated on March 17, 1936 (despite a historic flood that day), include a piece of the Blarney Stone from County Cork and stones from the White House sent by President Roosevelt. Father Cox wanted the Irish from "Shantytown" to empathize with Jesus as he walked the twenty-eight steps to Pontius Pilate, so he added a replica of twenty-eight granite stairs from the Vatican that worshipers ascend on their knees. St. Patrick's Church was a center of the city and center of Irish life for many generations. Today, the parish is merged with St. Stanislaus Church a few blocks away, but the people of St. Patrick's left their mark on America. And now, if you hear an old-timer say, "It looks like Cox's army has moved out!" you know they disapprove of someone's baggy and ill-fitting attire.

The Pittsburgh Kid

In a city that celebrates its teams and sports stars, there is only one "Pittsburgh Kid." The life of boxer Billy Conn could have been a successful movie plot. The son of Westinghouse Conn, a steelworker from East Liberty, Billy Conn was done with school at age fourteen; it simply did not suit him. Westinghouse Conn did not want his son working in the same mills that were destroying his health, but he also worried about his son running the streets and finding trouble. Consequently, he offered retired boxer Johnny Ray a dollar a week to start teaching boxing at the Lyceum in the lower Hill District. The Lyceum had been opened at 110 Washington Place by Father Lawrence O'Connell of the Epiphany Church to provide organized sports and supervised activities for Pittsburgh youth. The 125-pound Kid's dedication and inquisitiveness paid off, and from Pittsburgh's Lyceum his legendary career was launched. Sportswriter Angelo Prospero has succinctly explained why Conn became an icon:

> *His left jab was like a rapier and Joe Louis called his left hook, the fastest he had ever seen. His combinations were a staccato of lightning strikes, his defense was almost impenetrable. Outside of a soporific punch, he was the complete package, a dream fighter...Another reason for the greatness and high ranking of Billy Conn was the caliber of opposition he faced. He beat the champions, the contenders, the punchers, the cuties and the black fighters no one else wanted to face. From 1937–1941, he ducked no one.*

Acting as both trainer and manager, Johnny Ray had Conn start his career on the pro circuit because there was little to learn from fighting amateurs. One of the first things he learned was how little money there was for aspiring pros. Sleeping in flophouses and surviving on inexpensive Italian hoagies, he made the rounds, often pitted against older fighters who were past their prime but had skills that would challenge the Kid. Conn began to rack up victories, not as a knockout king but as a skillful boxer with fast legs and lightning punches who wore out his opponents. Soon he was a regular on the bill at Duquesne Gardens, pitted against both Pittsburgh favorites and national talents. The history of Conn's career is well documented elsewhere, and it will suffice to say that his career record was sixty-three wins (including fourteen knockouts), eleven losses and one draw. He defeated former or future champions such as Fritzie Zivic, Solly Kreiger, Teddy Yaroz and Young Corbett III.

Many consider 1939 to be the peak of Conn's career, when the "Pittsburgh Kid" bested Fred Apostoli, the "San Francisco Bellhop," in two matches at Madison Square Garden. The "Ham and Cabbage Express," chartered by Pittsburgh tavern owner Owney McManus, delivered hundreds of fans who smoked corncob pipes and sported green bowler hats in support of their hometown Irish pugilist. New York mobsters who tried to muscle in for a piece of the Pittsburgh Kid were compelled to back off by Art Rooney and his associates. The fights were spectacular, as were the exchanges of ethnic insults. In the fifteen-round rematch, the dialogue between the fighters and Conn's blue streak of cursing about Apostoli's dirty tricks were unprintable in the papers, but the microphone beneath the ring made the colorful exchanges audible to the first twelve rows of spectators. Conn was victorious by decision in both matches.

On July 13, 1939, Conn defeated the world light heavyweight champion, Melio Bettina, in a fifteen-round decision; successfully defended his title in a rematch; and defeated challenger Gus Lesnveich. Johnny Ray made plans for Conn to beef up and challenge the world heavyweight champion, Joe Louis, after Conn abdicated the lightweight championship and defeated the number-one heavyweight contender, Bob Pastor. This was also a good point in Conn's career to elope with Mary Louise Smith, daughter of the fiery-tempered Jimmy Smith. The hotheaded former second baseman for the 1917 World Championship New York Giants, Smith had declared, "I'll never allow that pug to marry my daughter."

Conn faced Louis in one of the greatest donnybrooks in boxing lore at Madison Square Garden on June 18, 1941. Pittsburghers arrived en masse and inebriated on the "Ham and Cabbage Express" or the "Shamrock Special." Conn had a clear lead for the first twelve rounds that he threw away when he attempted to knock out Louis. The Brown bomber knocked out Conn instead. When asked by a reporter why he went for the knockout, Conn famously quipped, "What's the point of being Irish if you can't be thick [stupid]?" Later, however, in an interview with Angelo Prospero, he said, "I found out before the fight my mom was terminally ill and I promised her a knockout." A 1941 movie, *The Pittsburgh Kid*, featured Conn playing himself, while a host of famous boxers filled out the cast. Although he had marquee looks, Conn was not a natural actor, and the movie, panned by critics, was trite and took liberties with his story.

The road to a rematch was detoured, first when Billy broke his hand in an altercation with his father-in-law, Jimmy Smith, and again when title boxing matches were suspended for the duration of World War II and both Louis and Conn entered military service. By the time of the long-awaited

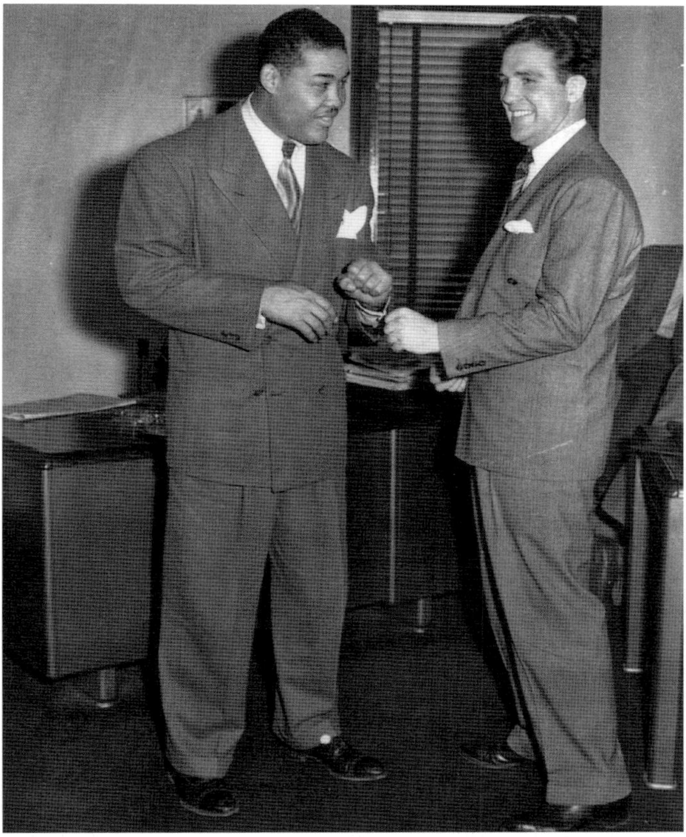

Joe Lewis (left) and Billy Conn (right). *Courtesy of Photo Antiquities.*

rematch on June 19, 1946, both Conn and Louis were no longer at their peaks, and Conn lost to Louis again after eight rounds. He retired from the ring, fighting a few exhibition matches. Thanks to savvy investment advice from Art Rooney, Conn never faced privation, unlike many retired boxers who wound up with nothing to show for their careers but scars. Conn did work briefly as a shill for Caesar's Palace, where he became good friends with Joe Louis, who had a similar gig there, and they are remembered for their banter. Conn would ask Louis, "Why couldn't you let me hold the title for a year or so?" and the Brown Bomber would reply, "You had the title for twelve rounds and you couldn't hold on to it."

Biographer Andrew O'Toole has pointed out another reason for Conn's enduring reputation: his media-friendly persona and rapport with reporters.

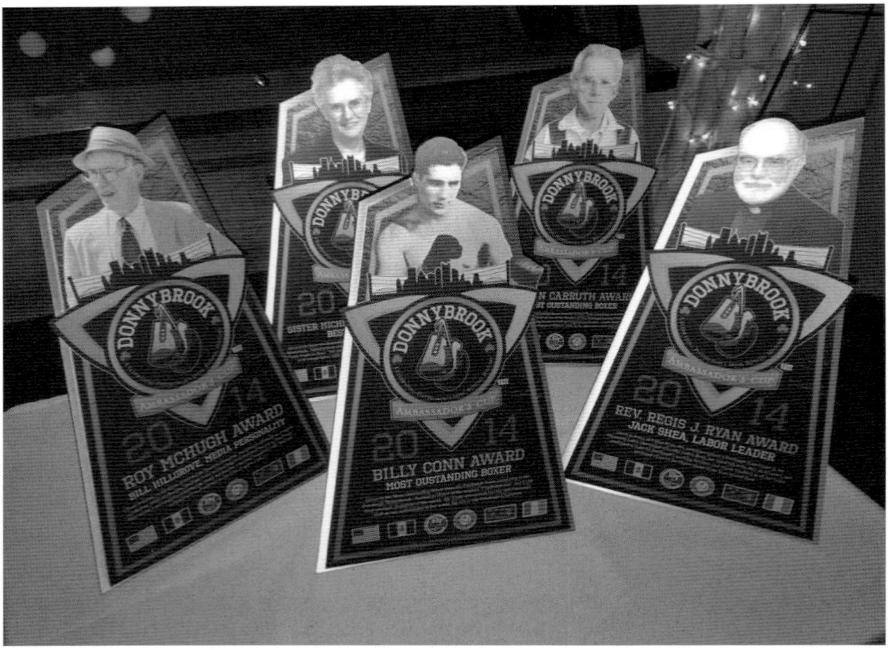

The Billy Conn Award. *Courtesy of the Ireland Institute of Pittsburgh.*

O'Toole states, "Conn was a newsman's delight. His answers weren't cluttered with diplomatically empty sound bites. Though he was deferential to his opponents, he answered questions honestly with any thought that came to mind. Billy simply held court while the enchanted reporters scribbled his brash and honest thoughts into their notebooks."

Long into retirement, Conn provided material for reporters, although his last notable fight had no judges or score. At age seventy-two, he stopped a convenience store robbery after the assailant punched the manager in the head. The would-be robber found himself brawling on the floor with Conn before finally running away. But Conn had taken hold of his coat, and the identification therein was used to catch the culprit. Conn died of cancer at age seventy-three in 1993, but he remains a Pittsburgh Irish legend, and a street in Oakland bears his name today. Conn is also honored and commemorated through the recently inaugurated Donnybrook Ambassador's Cup, a boxing match between Ireland and Pittsburgh held on March 17; the Billy Conn Award recognizes the most outstanding fighter from the Pittsburgh team.

Part VI
FINISHING TOUCHES

Renaissance and Reinvention, 1945–2015

Examining Pittsburgh's Irish community after World War II places us on a difficult-to-outline continuum from history to memory and finally to current events. Pittsburgh has been transformed from a "smoky old town" to a twenty-first-century metropolis without joining the ranks of rustbelt cities in the industrial North of the United States. Emmigration from Ireland continued, and Pittsburgh consistently ranks in America's top ten Irish cities, whether by ethnic self-identification or DNA analysis.

Reigning in the Radicals

In 1946, as the federal government lifted wartime controls that had banned striking while fixing prices and wages, a successful wave of strikes ensued in the steel, auto and electrical industries. A strong union environment in the postwar economic prosperity meant a rising standard of living for workers, and in 1949, Phillip Murray's steelworkers gained one of the first pension plans for industrial workers. After the war, however, Murray was also compelled to confront the issue of Communists in the CIO as the iron curtain descended and the Cold War began. Before Senator McCarthy and the anti-Communist "witch hunts" of the House Un-American Activities Committee grabbed headlines, Pittsburgh gained an early start on red-baiting due to the vigorous activities of Judge Michael

Musmanno. Pittsburgh's Irish labor priest Father Charles Owen Rice pushed Murray hard on the issue of eliminating Communists from union ranks.

Rice was a strong voice for social justice, but the Soviet's atheistic antagonism toward religion in general and the forced closure of churches and executions of clergymen in eastern bloc nations by Communists made any accommodation with them intolerable for Rice. The Soviet blockade of Berlin in 1948 marked a further ratcheting of Cold War tensions, while in domestic politics, the Communist Party's support for the Progressive Party threatened to throw the presidential election to the Republicans. In light of these developments, Murray supported Rice and anti-Communist union activist John Duffy in an all-out fight to break the Communist Party's power in the union movement. The effort led to the split of the United Electrical Workers (UE), the expulsion of the left-led unions from the CIO and the removal of some officials from the

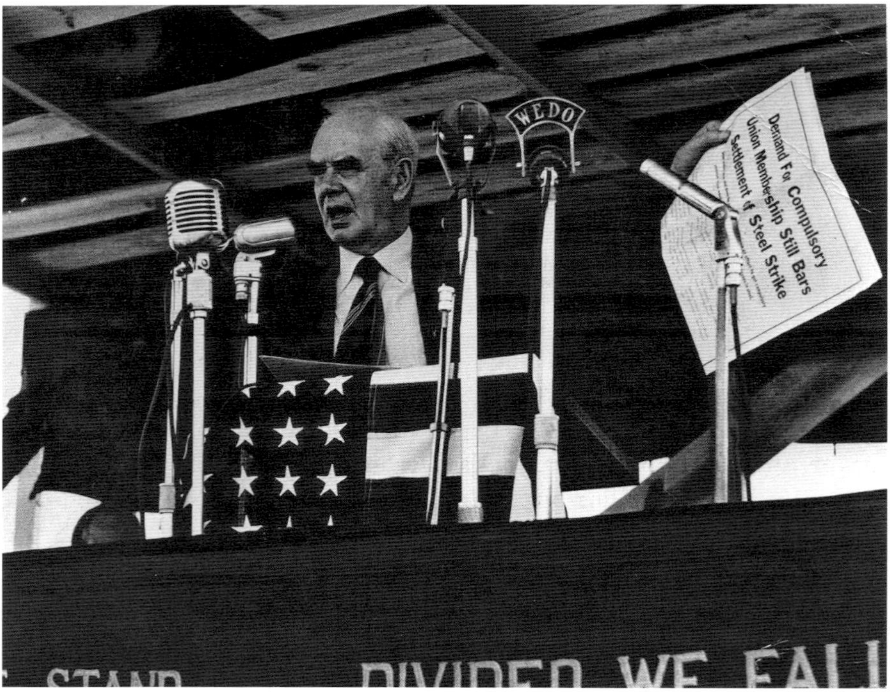

Phillip Murray shortly before his death in 1952. *Courtesy of Carnegie Library of Pittsburgh, Oakland.*

steelworkers' union. In short, as Cold War fears of Communism rose to a crescendo in the postwar years, labor leaders were compelled to enter into a Faustian bargain with management; in return for decent wages and job security, they would abandon radical agitation for social reform and eliminate the Communists, real or suspected, within their ranks. Murray died in 1952 on the campaign trail for Adlai Stevenson, never living to see the long-term death spiral of the steel industry in Pennsylvania.

Mayors N'at

Pittsburgh's Irish community contributed to a series of colorful mayors in the twentieth century. David L. Lawrence served as mayor of Pittsburgh from 1945 to 1958, when he became Pennsylvania's first Catholic governor. He was not the first Irish Catholic mayor of Pittsburgh, however; that distinction belongs to Bernard McKenna. McKenna, who had overseen the establishments of the Pittsburgh Zoo and Highland Park in the late 1890s, would have been impressed by the accomplishments of the urban renewal, known as the "Renaissance," under Lawrence that gave Pittsburgh its Gateway Center, Mellon Arena, Point State Park and a more efficient system of downtown bridges.

Pittsburgh mayor and gubernatorial candidate Peter F. Flaherty was the son of a Peter Flaherty who gave up farming rocks in Galway and immigrated to San Francisco. Unafraid to kick political sacred cows, Flaherty cut a decisive figure, taking on unions and nixing expensive proposals, such as Skybus, in the name of cutting costs. Long before Mayor Bob O'Connor urged us to "redd up Pittsburgh," Mayor Flaherty implored Pittsburghers to "Keep It Clean," but in this instance, the mayor and the department heads personally pitched in with garbage collection during a collectors' strike. Tom Murphy oversaw Pittsburgh's transformation into a technology center while struggling with the demographics of urban flight and the aftermath of two decades of mill closures; rails to trails conversions are a significant legacy of his administrations. Bob O'Connor served only eight months as mayor before succumbing to brain cancer on September 1, 2006, but there remains no shortage of Irish mayoral contenders in Pittsburgh.

Michael Francis Coyne rose from a blue-collar background to a successful political career and served two terms on city council before being elected

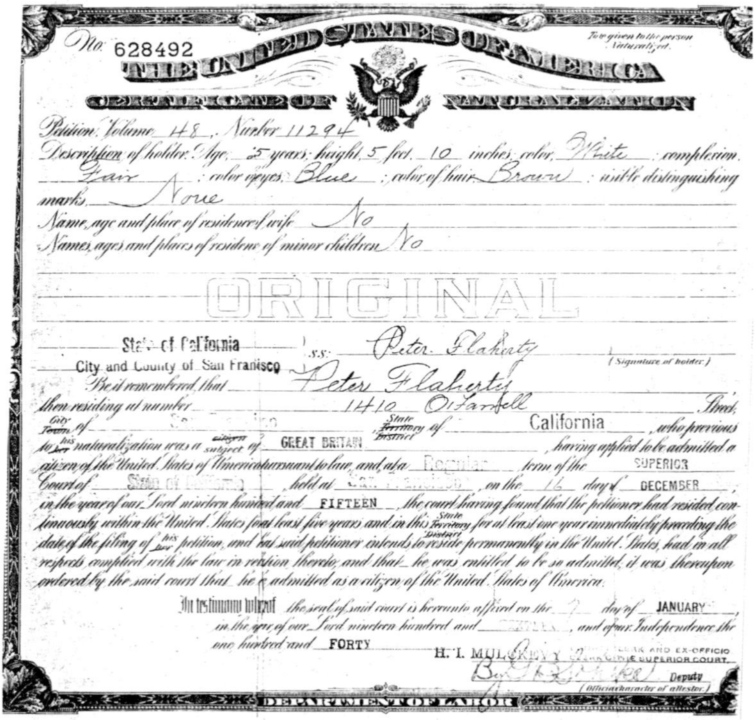

No. 628492

THE UNITED STATES OF AMERICA

CERTIFICATE OF NATURALIZATION

To be given to the person Naturalized.

Petition, Volume 48, Number 11294

Description of holder: Age, 25 years; height, 5 feet, 10 inches; color, White; complexion, Fair; color of eyes, Blue; color of hair, Brown; visible distinguishing marks, None

Name, age and place of residence of wife No

Names, ages and places of residence of minor children No

ORIGINAL

State of California } ss: Peter Flaherty (Signature of holder.)
City and County of San Francisco

Be it remembered, that Peter Flaherty then residing at number 1410 O'Farrell Street, City of San Francisco State of California, who previous to his naturalization was a subject of GREAT BRITAIN, having applied to be admitted a citizen of the United States of America pursuant to law, and at a Regular term of the SUPERIOR Court of State of California held at San Francisco on the 16 day of DECEMBER in the year of our Lord nineteen hundred and FIFTEEN, the court having found that the petitioner had resided continuously within the United States for at least five years and in this State for at least one year immediately preceding the date of the filing of his petition, and that said petitioner intends to reside permanently in the United States, had in all respects complied with the law in relation thereto, and that he was entitled to be so admitted, it was thereupon ordered by the said court that he be admitted as a citizen of the United States of America.

In testimony whereof the seal of said court is hereunto affixed on the 7 day of JANUARY in the year of our Lord nineteen hundred and SIXTEEN, and of our Independence the one hundred and FORTY

H. I. MULCREVY CLERK AND EX-OFFICIO CLERK OF THE SUPERIOR COURT.
By Deputy
(Official character of attestor.)

DEPARTMENT OF LABOR

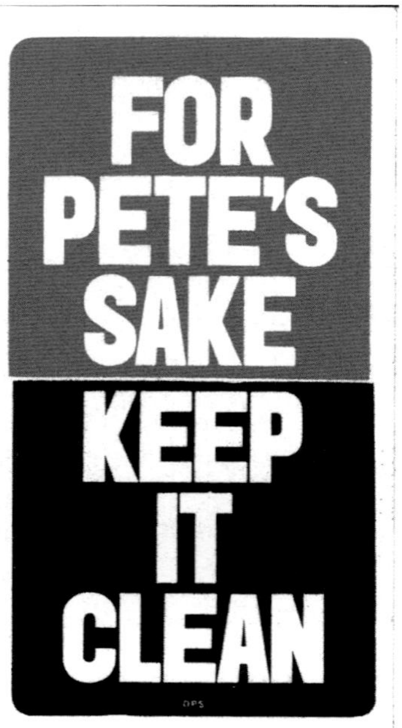

Above: Pete Flaherty's father's naturalization papers. *Courtesy of Archives Service Center, University of Pittsburgh.*

Left: Pete Flaherty slogan. *Courtesy of Archives Service Center, University of Pittsburgh.*

Allegheny County prothonotary in 1991. Coyne grew up in Hazelwood, where his father, Michael F. Coyne Sr., was a pipe fitter for the Baltimore and Ohio Railroad. His mother, Jeanne Morrison Coyne, was an organizer and local president for the Association of Federal, State, County and Municipal Employees. Michael Coyne sponsored legislation that prohibited the City of Pittsburgh from investing in companies in Northern Ireland that discriminated against Catholics.

His brother, Billy Coyne, represented Pittsburgh's Fourteenth Congressional District for twenty-two continuous years and was among the Pittsburgh politicians who supported Gerry Adams's visit to Pittsburgh in 1996. This was a groundbreaking event. Previously, leaders of Sinn Fein had been denied entry to the United States because the Reagan and Thatcher administrations considered them to be the political wing of the IRA and, hence, terrorists. The Clinton administration, supportive of the ongoing peace process in Northern Ireland, granted Adams a forty-eight-hour visa in January 1994. From that point on, Sinn Fein leaders

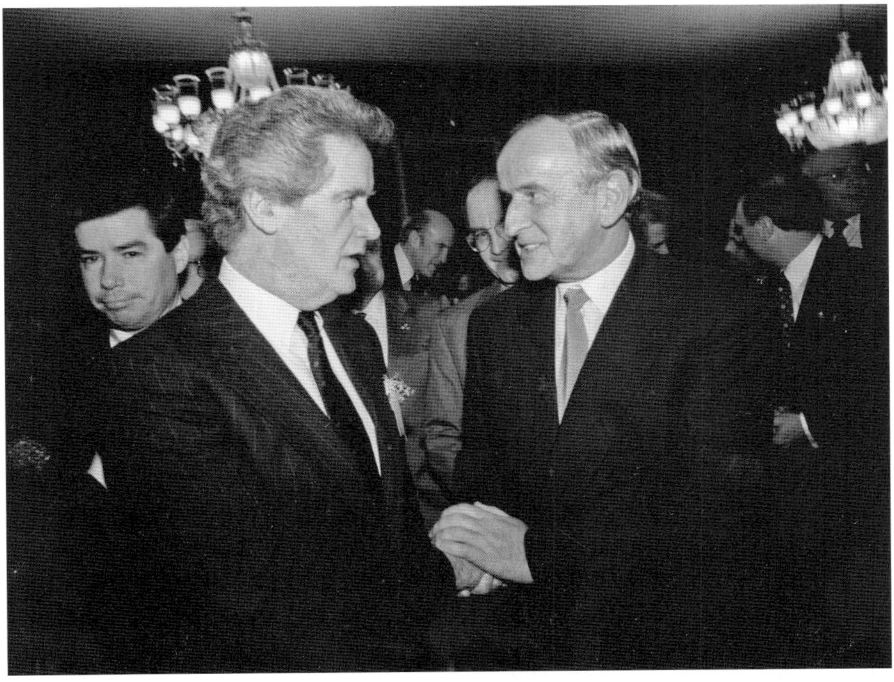

Billy Coyne (left) and Albert Reynolds. *Courtesy of the Ireland Institute of Pittsburgh.*

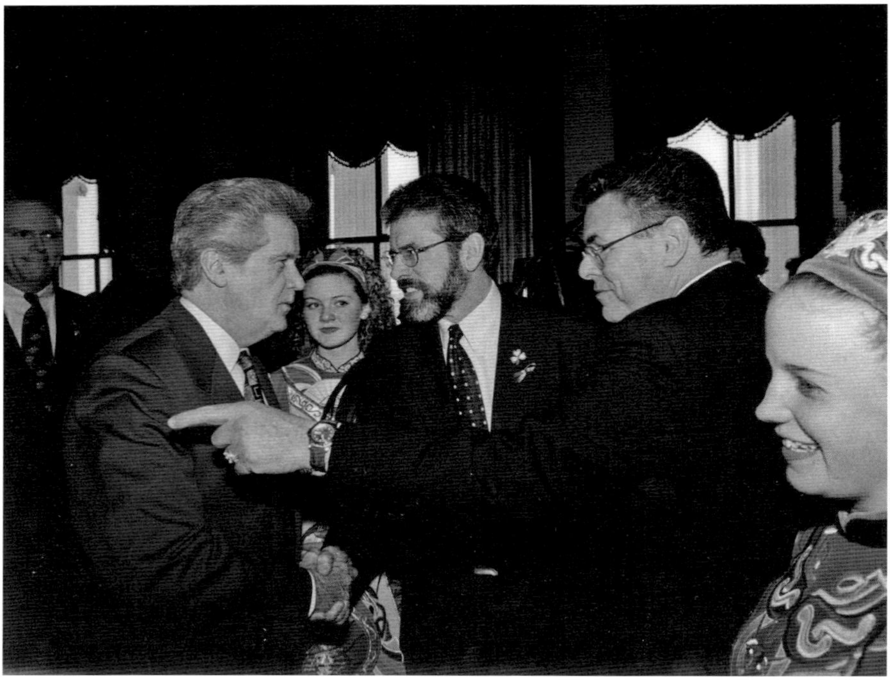

Left to right: Billy Coyne, Gerry Adams and Peter King. *Courtesy of the Ireland Institute of Pittsburgh.*

could directly and personally engage the American public. Irish political leaders in Pittsburgh continue to support the peace and reconciliation process in Ireland.

Twentieth-Century Global Connections

The American Irish Foundation was established by Irish president Eamon de Valera and U.S. president John F. Kennedy during Kennedy's June 1963 visit to Ireland. In 1976, Pittsburgh businessman Anthony J. O'Reilly of the Heinz Corporation and Dan Rooney, Steelers owner and former ambassador to Ireland, set up the Ireland Fund. Since St. Patrick's Day 1987, the two organizations have been merged as the Ireland Fund, which continues to promote community development, peace and reconciliation, arts and culture and education in the Republic of Ireland and Northern Ireland.

The Ireland Institute of Pittsburgh was established in 1989 by Sister Michele O'Leary, Dr. Mel Madden, Daniel M. Rooney and Dr. Anthony J. O'Reilly. Here, people from western Pennsylvania have taken practical and dramatic steps to promote mutual understanding between the Catholic and Protestant traditions and to contribute to the political, economic and social stability of Northern Ireland and the Republic of Ireland. Members of all political parties of Northern Ireland have been hosted in Pittsburgh, and the institute worked closely with the International Fund for Ireland, providing job-training opportunities in Pittsburgh to about two thousand people from Ireland in the past twenty-five years. Working with the U.S. State Department to implement the Walsh Visa program and similar opportunities such as the Wider Horizons Program, the institute enables young adults, often with limited educational background, to interact with Pittsburghers and experience working in America for Pittsburgh-based companies. Participants are largely drawn from Northern Ireland and the northern tier of counties in the Republic of Ireland.

This may seem like small potatoes, but Jim Lamb of the institute readily explains that their work indirectly affects the lives of countless additional thousands of families, co-workers and community members in Ireland,

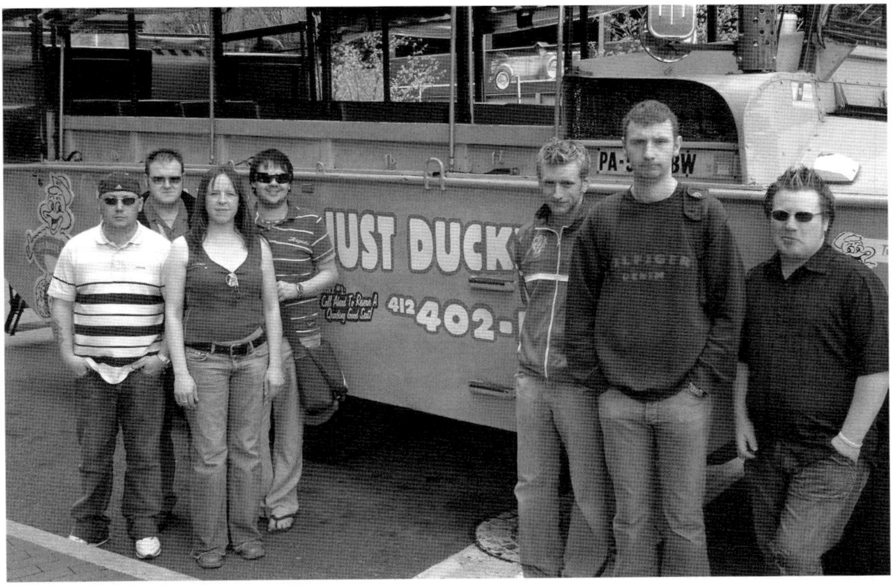

Ireland Institute Walsh Visa interns, Station Square, 2006. *Courtesy of the Ireland Institute of Pittsburgh.*

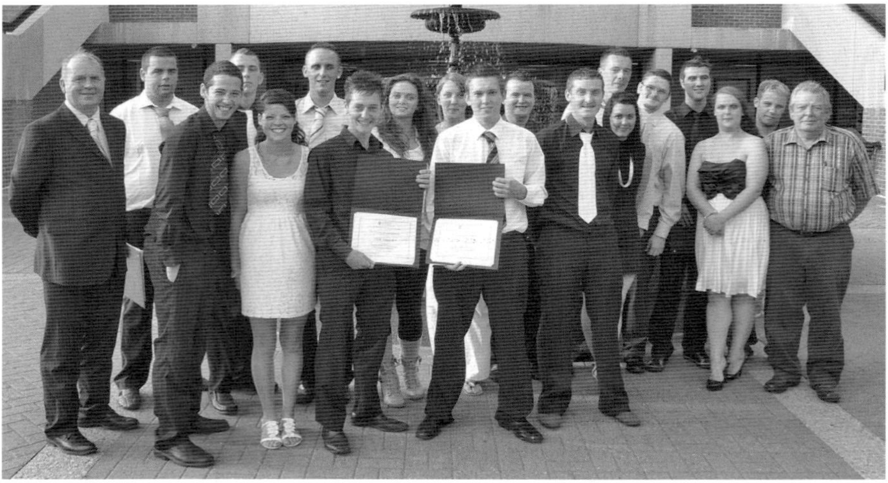

Ireland Institute's Duquesne graduates, 2010. *Courtesy of the Ireland Institute of Pittsburgh.*

which makes the program a remarkable achievement. Ultimately, change is wrought by interactions between individuals; governments and corporations are incapable of learning trust and open communication because they are simply machines created by humans. Our guests from conflict-ridden parts of Ireland learn new American perspectives in Pittsburgh, but just as importantly, they develop conflict resolution skills by communicating over small issues such as a messy roommate. The ability to resolve small problems gives hope for tackling larger issues.

The list of collaborations and cooperative efforts undertaken by the institute is far too lengthy to go through here; instead, we should, in keeping with its successful mission, briefly look at the experience of one individual in Pittsburgh. "Sean O'Neil" hailed from a "wee village" in Donegal, and although he was interested in working with youth, he was unemployed. The Wider Horizons Program placed him at the YMCA in Hazelwood, a disadvantaged neighborhood of Pittsburgh, where he gained practical experience and developed his cross-cultural communication skills. Living with a Pittsburgh Irish host family gave O'Neil a close-up view of American life and values. Returning to Ireland, graduates of the program have an impressive (for Ireland) employment rate of over 90 percent.

Since March 17, 2014, the Ireland Institute, along with the Hibernian Celtic Athletic Fund and the Western Pennsylvania Athletic League, has organized the Building Trades Donnybrook Ambassador's Cup. Held at the Priory on the Northside, this event pits local up-and-coming boxers against

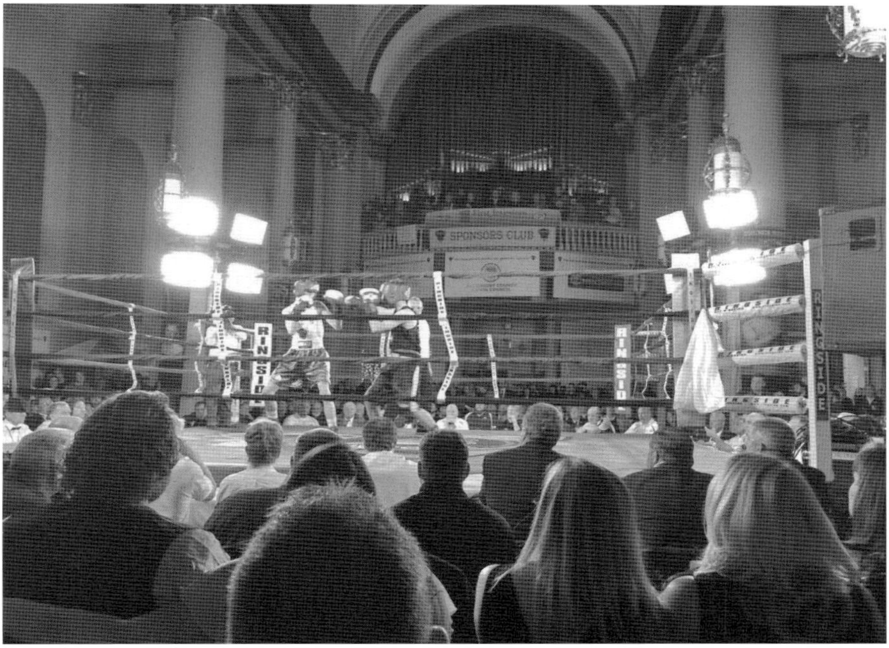

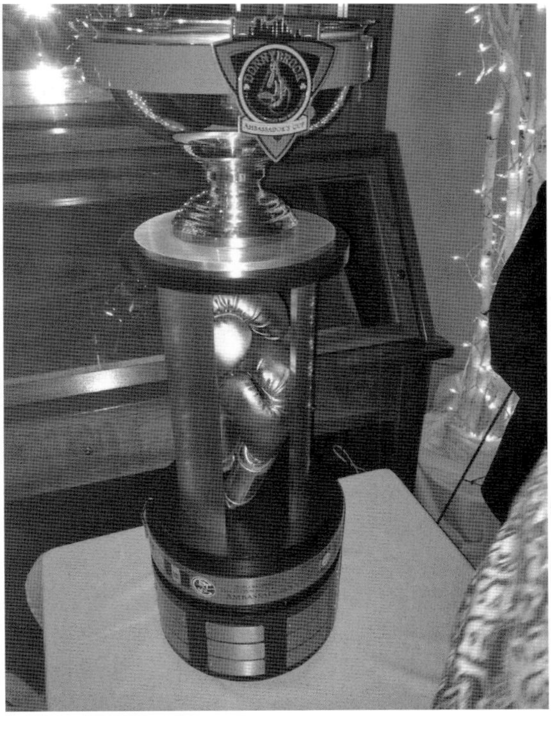

Above: The 2014 Donnybrook, held at the Priory. *Courtesy of the Ireland Institute of Pittsburgh.*

Right: The Donnybrook Ambassador's Cup. *Courtesy of the Ireland Institute of Pittsburgh.*

a team from Ireland in a demonstration of furious fighting and international sportsmanship. Pittsburgh is also home to the Pittsburgh Harlequins Rugby Team, founded in 1973 and based at Founder's Field in Cheswick. Another Irish sport, hurling, combines elements of hockey, soccer and baseball with football-style field goals, creating a fast-paced game; the small but growing Pittsburgh Hurling Club has promoted hurling in western Pennsylvania since 2003 and now fields the Pittsburgh Pucas. While Pittsburgh's Irish community participates in other sports too numerous to mention, it is fitting that the three rivers would have an Irish Rowing Club.

Three Rivers Dance

Irish dancing, brought to a wider audience by shows such as *Riverdance* and *Michael Flatley's Lord of the Dance*, has a long history and a strong sense of tradition. Pittsburgh's traditional Irish dance scene has its roots in the late 1960s, when dancers from places like Wilkinsburg and Swissvale carpooled on Saturdays to take their lessons from Miss Maureen Kearney at the AOH in Homestead. Aside from Irish jig contests such as those held at AOH events earlier in the twentieth century, competition dancing was largely unknown at the time, and most people danced in the privacy of their homes. Cleveland had started its dance festival (*feis*) in 1956, and Bob Masterson, an Irish dance teacher in Cleveland, began teaching classes in Pittsburgh prior to 1970, but he generally delegated instruction to his students. Although they were probably quite good, they were not certified, and parents were increasingly interested in having certified teachers registered with the governing body in Ireland.

The Gaelic League (Conradh na Gaeilge) was founded in Dublin in 1893 to promote Irish culture, with an emphasis on language and literature. Its first *céilí* was held in 1897 in London and the first *feis* in Macroom in 1898. By the early 1920s, both Cork and Leinster had their own teachers, and Irish dancing had become popular throughout Ireland. The league pushed for and supported the Irish Dancing Commission (An Coimisiún le Rincí Gaelacha), which first met in June 1930 as the authority charged with regulating Irish dancing affairs. The commission, often abbreviated as TCRG, developed an examination system for teachers of Irish dancing in 1943 and subsequently developed certifications for judges and teachers of team (*céilí*) dancing, but until the late 1960s, it legislated almost exclusively for Irish dancing in Ireland. This change to a global perspective from the late 1960s onward was evident in the Pittsburgh area.

Events in Pittsburgh coincided with the introduction of the World Irish Dancing Championships (Oireachtas Rince na Cruinne) in 1970. This was arguably the single most important development in Irish dancing in the eighty-year history of the commission, which was consequently transformed from a national legislative body to a global body. Since 2000, the World Championship has been held outside the Republic of Ireland, in Belfast, Glasgow and Philadelphia. Up to the 1980s, meetings of the commission were conducted entirely in Gaelic, but this gradually changed to accommodate the ever-increasing representation of regions outside Ireland. Nonetheless, the Irish language continued to be actively encouraged, and some of the examinations for proficiency retained an Irish language component. The commission's main objectives remained preservation and promotion of Irish dancing, including step-dancing and team dancing. Competing at festivals (*feiseanna*) required regular instruction by a certified teacher.

In late 1970, a delegation that included Pete Shovlin traveled to Cleveland on behalf of the Irish Centre of Pittsburgh to confer with Theresa "Tessie" Burke, who was also an Irish dance teacher in Cleveland with TCRG certification. It was arranged that Burke would begin teaching Irish dance classes to the children of the members of the Irish Centre. Out of Burke's classes in Pittsburgh, two dance schools were started by former students: the Shovlin Academy of Irish Dance and the Bell School of Irish Dance. Burke's school continues to this day as the Burke-Conroy School of Irish Dance. Two former students, Mary and Laura Conroy, are now teaching with her.

Many dancers from the Irish Centre started competing that summer, and Pittsburgh held its first *feis* in July 1971. A quick way to get Pittsburgh's dancers in costume for that first summer was to purchase the old Burke school costumes, as the Burke school was in the process of changing its dance outfit. That costume was the light powder blue dress seen at many early performances by the Shovlin Academy, but about two years later, it was replaced by a forest green outfit with embroidery. The Irish Centre of Pittsburgh has hosted the Pittsburgh Feis every year since 1971, and its committee now organizes three *feisanna* each year to promote this exciting and evolving dance form.

Dancers' costumes have changed over time as well, becoming more elaborate, not due to outside influences or increased popularity but largely because less expensive methods than tedious hand embroidery are available.

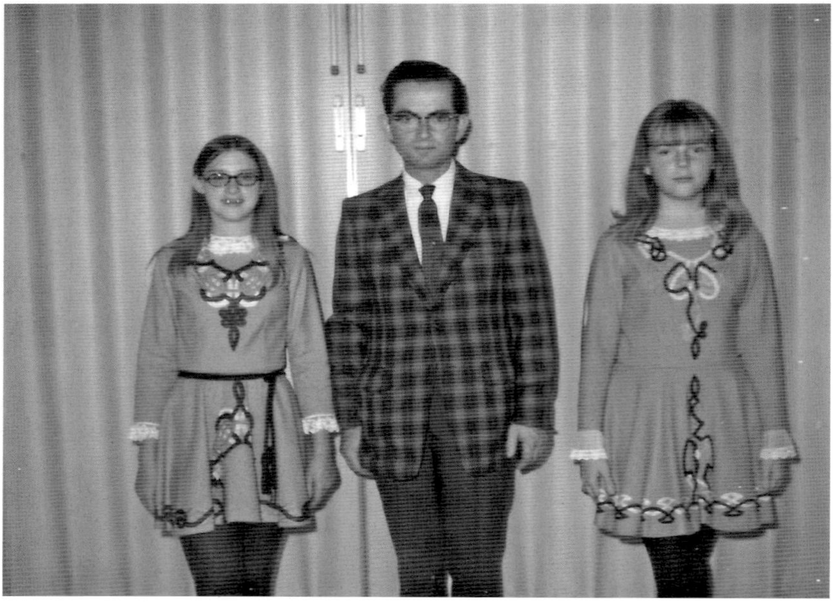

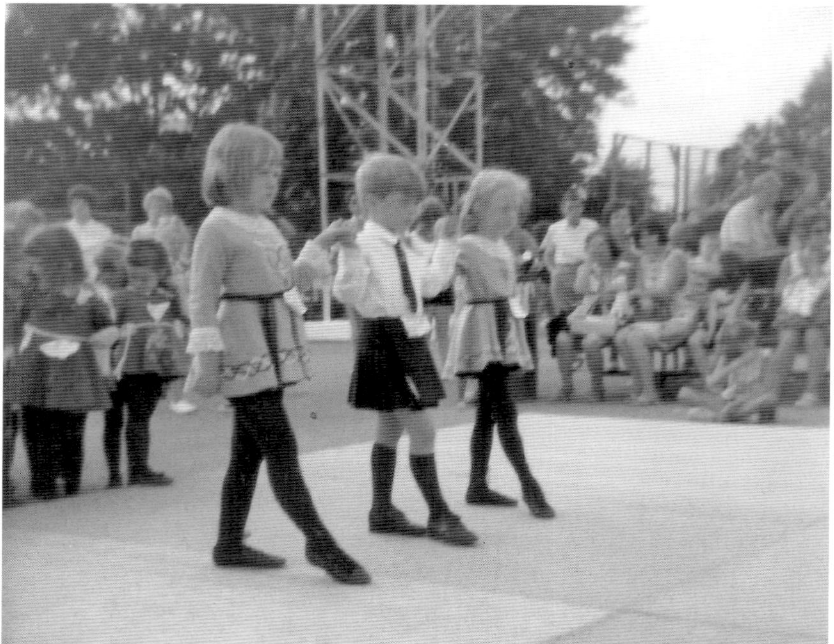

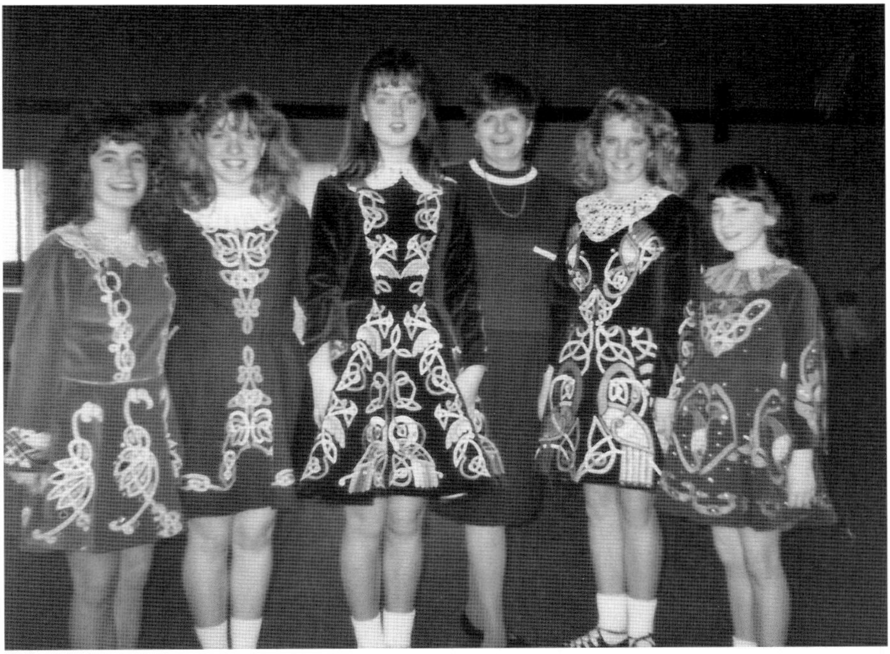

Shovlin academy dancers, 1988. *Courtesy of Liz Shovlin Grinko.*

Opposite, top: Shovlin Academy dancers, 1971. *Courtesy of Liz Shovlin Grinko.*

Opposite, bottom: Shovlin Academy of Dance, Detroit Feis, 1971. *Courtesy of Liz Shovlin Grinko.*

The solo costumes worn by individual dancers do remain expensive, as each one is unique. Maggie and Sally Folan of the Pittsburgh Irish Reelers were also students of Bob Masterson, and today they teach and promote Irish dancing. Since 1990, the Pittsburgh Ceili Club has promoted traditional forms of Irish social dancing, known as *ceili* and set dancing and accompanied by live music in the Irish folk tradition. Pittsburgh's Irish dancers are part of a global network of Irish dancers, and their teachers regularly share their knowledge and enjoyment of this rich culture. Dancers continue to be accompanied by Irish music played on traditional instruments, such as accordion, piano, fiddle, flute, banjo and occasionally uilleann pipes. Irish dancing, once the traditional dance form of Ireland, is now popular in unexpected places, such as Japan, Brazil, Argentina and Eastern Europe.

CONCLUSION

After World War II, the Irish continued to immigrate to Pittsburgh, often via Canada, working in the trades as painters, plasterers, plumbers and domestics. Others were entrepreneurs who built successful businesses in construction or in the hospitality and service industries. Following established patterns, many became firemen, policemen and utility workers. They married other Irish, Germans and Italians, and today, many Irish Pittsburghers are second and third generations of mixed ancestry. A new cause of immigration in the early 1970s was "the Troubles," a wave of violence in Northern Ireland. Some did not flee but sent their children to relatives in Pittsburgh, a modern instance of chain migration. Today, fallout from the economic crisis of 2008 and the International Monetary Fund's mandates of "austerity" again compel the sons and daughters of Ireland to depart for better opportunities in places like Pittsburgh.

The Irish Centre of Pittsburgh in Squirrel Hill was created in the 1960s and remains a cultural institution promoting Gaelic arts and music. From its inception, the centre has hosted distinguished visitors from Ireland, including several prime ministers (*taoiseachs*). There is, however, a bit of irony in the era that saw the completion of the Irish Centre; the same prosperity and assimilation that facilitated the construction of new ethnic community centers undercut community participation. Many Irish Americans either lost interest in things Irish or their support for Irish fraternal organizations declined because, once integrated into American society, they had other communal options. Other ethnic communities faced similar declines in

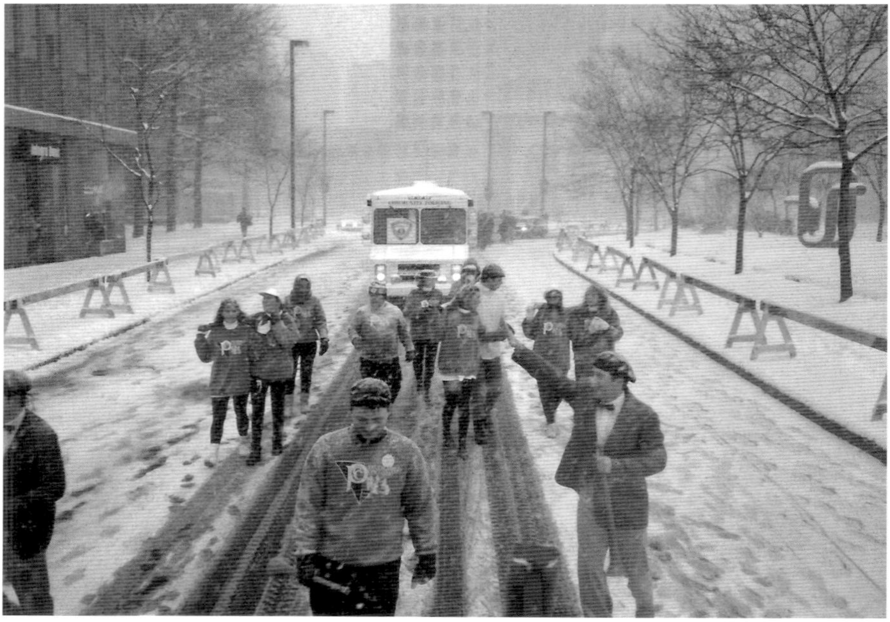

Festive marchers in the "Blizzard Parade" of 1993. *Courtesy of Liz Shovlin Grinko.*

participation. Since the 1970s, the AOH has attracted the attention and support of a younger generation and has rebounded from a decidedly low point. One striking demonstration of the dedication of Irish Pittsburgh was the famous "Blizzard Parade" of 1993, in which Irish policemen, musicians, dancers and civic associations marched despite the severe weather and entreaties from authorities to desist in the interest of public safety. Getting home from the parade turned out to be the tricky part, and there are many tales of three-day "hooleys" following the parade, as out-of-town guests had no way to leave after two feet of snow shut down the city. Western Pennsylvania's Irish community continues to support an enormous range of philanthropic and cultural institutions, Irish pubs and retail stores, festivals, theatrical performances, sports clubs and, of course, musicians.

It is said that all history is contemporary history and, furthermore, that it contains strong autobiographical elements that influence an author's interpretation of events, indeed even the selection of events to be examined. There is simply no way to cover every major event in the long arc of Irish Pittsburgh's history, much less present various interpretations of all these events. This has been my story in a sense, presenting a glimpse of Irish

Pittsburgh from a particular point of view; however, the value of recognizing divergent viewpoints cannot be overestimated. For instance, in order for the Good Friday Agreement to work and bring peace to Northern Ireland, the various parties had to accede to the existence of two incompatible narratives while simultaneously acknowledging both viewpoints as being legitimate. At the same time the agreement acknowledged that the majority of the people of Northern Ireland wished to remain a part of the United Kingdom, it simultaneously acknowledged that a substantial section of the people of Northern Ireland, and the majority of the people of the island of Ireland, wished to bring about a united Ireland.

In a similar fashion, I encourage readers to listen for other narratives, both within the written word and without. Many elements found in this story speak to American identity as well as the Irish experience in America, and a considerable amount of lore was encountered in the process of creating this work. Moreover, the emphasis on labor and employment in the history of Irish Pittsburgh is arguably due to an innate American tendency to value employment in identity construction. Likewise, the story's staggering depiction of violence is clearly reflective of American society.

Walking the streets of Pittsburgh and the hills and hollows of western Pennsylvania, we can sense that history lies at our feet (quite literally in the case of the forgotten canal tunnel under Grant's Hill that was built by Irish hands almost two hundred years ago). It is my hope that books such as this one will help readers see our city in a new light and start new conversations about who we are and how we came to be here.

An Deireadh

SELECTED BIBLIOGRAPHY

Archival Materials

Ancient Order of Hibernians Records. MSS 351, John Heinz History Center, Detre Library and Archives, Pittsburgh, PA.

Catholic Historical Society Records. Duquesne University Archives, Gumberg Library, Pittsburgh, PA.

Collins, John B. John B. Collins Papers, 1913–1976. AIS.1977.17, Archives Service Center, University of Pittsburgh, PA.

Cox, James. Papers of Father James Cox. St. Patrick–St. Stanislaus Kostka Parish Archives, Pittsburgh, PA.

Flaherty, Peter F. Peter F. Flaherty Papers. AIS.1999.19, Archives Service Center, University of Pittsburgh, PA.

McKenna, Charles F. Civil War Letters to His Family. Transcribed by Gerard F. O'Neil, 2009. Soldiers and Sailors Memorial Hall Archives, Pittsburgh, PA.

O'Brien, Edward. Paper of Edward O'Brien. MSS 390, John Heinz History Center, Detre Library and Archives, Pittsburgh, PA.

Articles

Adams, James H. "The Negotiated Hibernian: Discourse on the Fenian in England and America." *American Nineteenth Century History* 11, no. 1 (March 2010).

SELECTED BIBLIOGRAPHY

Allison, Milton M. "Iffly: 'Ghost Town.'" *Western Pennsylvania Historical Magazine* 35, no. 2 (June 1952).

Bankhurst, Benjamin. "A Looking-Glass for Presbyterians: Recasting a Prejudice in Late Colonial Pennsylvania." *Pennsylvania Magazine of History and Biography* 133, no. 4 (October 2009).

Betten, Neil. "Charles Owen Rice: Pittsburgh Labor Priest, 1936–1940." *Pennsylvania Magazine of History and Biography* 94, no. 4 (October 1970).

Bruce, Susannah Ural. "'Remember Your Country and Keep Up Its Credit': Irish Volunteers and the Union Army, 1861–1865." *Journal of Military History* 69, no. 2 (April 2005).

Coode, Thomas, and John D. Petrarulo. "The Odyssey of Pittsburgh's Father Cox." *Western Pennsylvania Historical Magazine* 55, no. 3 (July 1972).

Craig, John M. "'There Is Hell Going On Up There': The Carnegie Klan Riot of 1923." *Pennsylvania History* 72, no. 3 (Summer 2005).

Daily Morning Post. "From the 'Seat of War.'" February 12, 1852.

———. "The Irish Riots at Steubenville." February 11, 1852.

Doyle, David Noel. "The Irish as Urban Pioneers in the United States, 1850–1870." *Journal of American Ethnic History* 10, no. 1 (Fall 1990–Winter 1991).

Gilmore, Peter. "'A Fiddler Was a Great Acquisition to Any Neighborhood': Traditional Music and Ulster Culture on the Pennsylvania Frontier." *Western Pennsylvania History* 83, no. 3 (Fall 2000).

Heinenman, Kenneth J. "A Catholic New Deal: Religion and Labor in 1930s Pittsburgh." *Pennsylvania Magazine of History and Biography* 118, no. 4 (October 1994).

———. "Iron City Trinity: The Triumph and Trials of Catholic Social Activism in Pittsburgh 1932–1972." *U.S. Catholic Historian* 22, no. 2, Urbanism and American Religion (Spring 2004).

Janis, Ely M. "Petticoat Revolutionaries: Gender, Ethnic Nationalism, and the Irish Ladies Land League in the United States." *Journal of American Ethnic History* 27, no. 2 (Winter 2008).

Kenny, Kevin. "Diaspora and Comparison: The Global Irish as Case Study." *Journal of American History* 90, no. 1 (June 2003).

McGough, Michael. "Feeble Opinions on the House Chaplaincy." *Religion in the News* 3, no. 2 (Summer 2000).

Meyerhuber, Carl I., Jr. "The Alle-Kiski Coal Wars, 1913–1919." *Western Pennsylvania Historical Magazine* 63, no. 2 (July 1980).

New York Times. "Fatal War Among Races: Irishmen and Italians Cracking Each Other's Skulls." September 20, 1886.

———. "Klan Riot Inquiry Balked at Carnegie." August 28, 1923.

Nolan, Janet. "Silent Generations: New Voices of Irish America." *American Literary History* 17, no. 3, Symposium Issue: Race, Ethnicity and Civic Identity in the Americas (Autumn 2005).

Pittsburgh Daily Gazette and Advertiser. "The Steubenville Rioters." February 16, 1852.

Porter, Gerald. "Big John—The Musical and Visual Iconography of the Male Worker." *Lore & Language* 12, Special Issue: Images, Identities and Ideologies, Papers from the 22nd International Ballad Conference, June 29–July 3, 1992, Belfast (Summer 1994).

Powers, Tom, and James Wudarczyk. "Arsenal Explosion." *Western Pennsylvania History* 96, no. 2 (Summer 2013).

Rafferty, Oliver. "Fenianism in North America in the 1860s: The Problem for Church and State." *Journal of the Historical Association* 84, no. 274 (1999).

Ridner, Judith. "Relying on the 'Saucy' Men of the Backcountry: Middlemen and the Fur Trade in Pennsylvania." *Pennsylvania Magazine of History and Biography* 129, no. 2 (April 2005).

Rowland, Thomas J. "Irish-American Catholics and the Quest for Respectability in the Coming of the Great War, 1900–1917." *Journal of American Ethnic History* 15, no. 2 (Winter 1996).

Walsh, Victor A. "Across 'The Big Wather': The Irish Catholic Community of Mid-Nineteenth-Century Pittsburgh." *Pennsylvania Magazine of History and Biography* 66, no. 1 (January 1983).

———. "'Drowning the Shamrock': Drink, Teetotalism, and the Irish Catholics of Gilded-Age Pittsburgh." *Journal of American Ethnic History* 10, no. 1 (Fall 1990–Winter 1991).

———. "'A Fanatic Heart': The Cause of Irish-American Nationalism in Pittsburgh During the Gilded Age." *Journal of Social History* 15, no. 2 (Winter 1981).

Weber, Michael P. "Residential and Occupational Patterns of Ethnic Minorities in Nineteenth Century Pittsburgh." *Pennsylvania History* 44, no. 4 (October 1977).

Books

Barrett, James R. *The Irish Way: Becoming American in the Multiethnic City*. New York: Penguin Press, 2012.

Bates, Samuel P. *History of Pennsylvania Volunteers, 1861–5; Prepared in Compliance with Acts of the Legislature*. Harrisburg, PA: B. Singerly, State Printer, 1869.

Beito, David T. *From Mutual Aid to the Welfare State: Fraternal Societies and Social Services, 1890–1967*. Chapel Hill: University of North Carolina Press, 2000.

Brackenridge, Hugh Henry. *Modern Chivalry*. New York: Hafner Publishing Company, 1968.

Catholic Historical Society of Western Pennsylvania. *Catholic Pittsburgh's One Hundred Years 1843–1943*. Chicago: Loyola University Press, 1943.

Centennial Atlas of Allegheny County. Philadelphia: G.M. Hopkins & Co., 1876.

Couvares, Francis G. *The Remaking of Pittsburgh: Class and Culture in an Industrializing City, 1877–1919*. Albany, NY: State University of Albany Press, 1984.

Dunbar Historical Society. *Dunbar*. Charleston, SC: Arcadia Publishing, 2009.

Dunne, Robert. *Antebellum Irish Immigration and Emerging Ideologies of "America": A Protestant Backlash*. Lewistown, NY: Edwin Mellen Press, 2002.

Fleming, George T. *"Flem's" Views of Old Pittsburgh: A Portfolio of the Past Precious with Memories*. Pittsburgh, PA: G.T. Fleming, 1905.

Fox, William F. *Regimental Losses in the Civil War, 1861–1865*. Albany, NY: Albany Publishing Company, 1889.

Gilmore, Peter E. *Rebels and Revivals: Ulster Immigrants, Western Pennsylvania Presbyterianism and the Formation of Scotch-Irish Identity*. Ann Arbor: University of Michigan Dissertation Services, 2009.

Hoerr, John. *Harry, Tom and Father Rice: Accusation and Betrayal in America's Cold War*. Pittsburgh, PA: University of Pittsburgh Press, 2005.

Hogeland, William. *The Whiskey Rebellion: George Washington, Alexander Hamilton, and the Frontier Rebels Who Challenged America's Newfound Sovereignty*. New York: Simon and Schuster, 2006.

Kleinberg, S.J. *The Shadow of the Mills: Working-Class Families in Pittsburgh, 1870–1907*. Pittsburgh, PA: University of Pittsburgh Press, 1989.

Klett, Guy S. *Presbyterians in Colonial Pennsylvania*. Philadelphia: University of Pennsylvania Press, 1937.

Knobel, Dale T. *Paddy and the Republican: Ethnicity and Nationality in Antebellum America*. Middletown, CT: Wesleyan University Press, 1986.

Korson, George Gershon. *Coal Dust on the Fiddle: Songs and Stories of the Bituminous Industry*. Philadelphia: University of Philadelphia Press, 1943.

———. *Pennsylvania Songs and Legends*. Philadelphia: University of Philadelphia Press, 1949.

Long, David. *The Rise and Fall of the Ku Klux Klan in Western Pennsylvania*. Ann Arbor: University of Michigan Dissertation Services, 1999.

Lorant, Stefan. *Pete: The Life of Pete Flaherty*. Boston: Nimrod Press, 1978.

———, ed. *Pittsburgh: The Story of an American City*. Lenox, MA: Authors Editions, Inc., 1975.

Martin, Scott C. "The Great Brothel Dousing: Leisure, Reform and Urban Change in Antebellum Pittsburgh." In *American Cities and Towns: Historical Perspectives*, edited by Joseph Rishel. Pittsburgh, PA: Duquesne University Press, 1992.

McCollester, Charles J. *The Point of Pittsburgh: Production and Struggle at the Forks of the Ohio*. Pittsburgh, PA: Battle of Homestead Foundation, 2008.

McGivern, Elaine Patricia. *Ethnic Identity and Its Relation to Group Norms: Irish Americans in Metropolitan Pittsburgh*. Ann Arbor: University of Michigan Dissertation Services, 1984.

Milano, Kenneth W. *The Philadelphia Riots: Irish Kensington Erupts*. Charleston, SC: The History Press, 2013.

Miller, Kirby A., Arnold Schrier, Bruce D. Boling and David D. Doyle, eds. *Irish Immigrants in the Land of Canaan: Letters and Memoirs from Colonial and Revolutionary America, 1675–1815*. New York: Oxford University Press, 2003.

Perry, Jay Martin. *Shillelaghs, Shovels, and Secrets: Irish Immigrant Secret Societies and the Building of Indiana Internal Improvements, 1835–1837*. Ann Arbor: University of Michigan Dissertation Services, 2010.

Rishel, Joseph A. *Founding Families of Pittsburgh*. Pittsburgh, PA: University of Pittsburgh Press, 1990.

———. *"The Spirit that Gives Life": The History of Duquesne University, 1878–1996*. Pittsburgh, PA: Duquesne University Press, 1997.

Steffens, Lincoln. *The Shame of the Cities*. New York: Hill and Wang, 1957.

Szarniki, Reverend Henry A. *Michael O'Connor: First Catholic Bishop of Pittsburgh, 1843–1860*. Pittsburgh, PA: Wolfson Publishing, 1975.

United States Army, Pennsylvania Infantry Regiment, 155th (1862–1865). *Under the Maltese Cross: Antietam to Appomattox the Loyal Uprising in Western Pennsylvania, 1861–1865; Campaigns 155th Pennsylvania Regiment*. Pittsburgh, PA: 155th Regimental Association, 1910.

Walsh, Victor Anthony. *Across "The Big Wather": Irish Community Life in Pittsburgh and Allegheny County*. Ann Arbor: University of Michigan Dissertation Services, 1995.

Weaver, Emily M. *The Fort Pitt Block House*. Charleston, SC: The History Press, 2013.

Woodard, Colin. *American Nations: A History of the Eleven Rival Regional Culture of North America*. New York: Penguin Books, 2011.

Songs

Feeney, Anne. "Fannie Sellins." Compact disc, 2003.
Mahoney, Jerry. "They Were All Far Downs but Me." Vinyl disc. New York: Celtic Music, n.d.
O'Connell, Robbie. "You're Not Irish." Compact disc. Celtic Media, 1998.

Websites

An Coimisiun Le Rinci Gaelaca—The Irish Dancing Commission. www.clrg.ie.
Historical Society of Pennsylvania. "Excerpt from 'Riots on Railways,' published in *The Irish American* on February 21, 1852." Exploring Diversity in Pennsylvania History. hsp.org/sites/default/files/railroadriot_revised.pdf.
Kincaid, David. "The 116th Regiment Pennsylvania Volunteers: A Brief History." www.hauntedfieldmusic.com/116th.html.
Maryniak, Benedict. "The Fenian Raid and the Battle of Ridgeway, June 1–3, 1866." www.acsu.buffalo.edu/~dbertuca/155/FenianRaid.html.
Prospero, Angelo. "Billy Conn—The One and Only Pittsburgh Kid." www.billyconn.net/articles/BILLY_CONN_the_one_and_only_Pgh_kid.htm.

INDEX

ABOUT THE AUTHOR

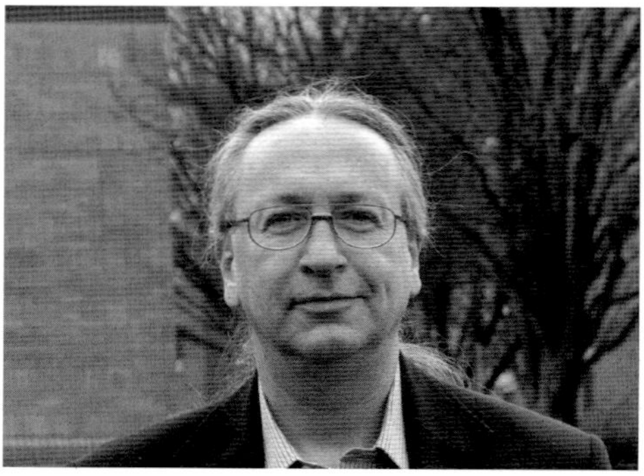

Gerard O'Neil has lived in the Pittsburgh area for over twenty years and has an MA in public history from Duquesne University, where he currently works as an archivist. In addition to working at the Writers' Center at La Roche College, he also provides sound systems for numerous cultural events in the Pittsburgh area. He has worked with many Irish bands and organizations in his capacity as a sound engineer, helping them bring the sounds of Ireland to Pittsburgh.